We are in Walter Strickland's debt for publishing a new edition of Charles Boothe's *Plain Theology for Plain People*, an extraordinary book by an extraordinary man. This is everyday theology from the margins, from below, from the perspective of the dispossessed. It is no dry textbook, but theology written by an African-American pastor, born into slavery, who sought to instruct ordinary people in the Christian faith. A classic volume, short, readable, informative, by an inspiring Christian leader.

—Michael F. Bird
Lecturer in Theology at Ridley College.

Any given Sunday in some black churches, a member of the congregation may encourage the pastor by saying, "Make it plain, preacher!" In *Plain Theology for Plain People*, Charles Octavius Boothe makes plain a systematic theology that is both faithful to biblical orthodoxy and responsive to the particular interests of black Christians. I am thankful to God that Walter Strickland discovered this literary jewel and now shares it with the contemporary people of the Lord. Too often, the black church is mischaracterized as being emotionally rich and intellectually shallow. *Plain Theology* shows this to be a harmful stereotype. All disciples of Jesus Christ interested in how to, in the words of Robert Smith Jr., make doctrine dance should read this book and apply it to the preaching of the plain and pure gospel of the Lord Jesus Christ.

—CJ Rhodes
Pastor of Mount Helm Baptist Church in Jackson, Mississippi.

By reprinting ... a book written for the average sharecropper, Walter R. Strickland has provided Christians with a helpful biblical and theological resource. Along with Strickland's insightful introduction, this book's reprinting provides another example (among many) of the contributions of black Christians to Christianity, their contributions to evangelical biblical and theological discourse, and their contributions to the intellectual environment of evangelical Christianity. Readers of Boothe's work will especially appreciate his intentional efforts to make the bible and theology accessible to his original audience.

—Jarvis J. Williams
Associate Professor of New Testament Interpretation at The Southern Baptist Theological Seminary.

Plain Theology for Plain People

Plain Theology for Plain People

Charles Octavius Boothe

Introduction by Walter R. Strickland II

LEXHAM PRESS

Plain Theology for Plain People

Copyright 2017 Lexham Press

Lexham Press, 1313 Commercial St., Bellingham, WA 98225
LexhamPress.com

Originally published by the American Baptist Publication Society, Philadelphia, 1890.

Print ISBN 9781683590347
Digital ISBN 9781683590668

Contents

– Introduction to Plain Theology for Plain People

Walter R. Strickland II

Charles Octavius Boothe (1845–1924) was a reluctant teacher. To spare others his frustration with learning and teaching from books laced with dense theological rhetoric, Boothe wrote *Plain Theology for Plain People*.[1]

Boothe wrote for the average sharecropper. He accommodated an unlearned audience that included pastors, teachers, and community leaders born into poverty with little access to education. While leaders and laity alike desperately needed biblical and theological truth, they had little time, energy, and resources to pursue education. "The doctrines of our holy religion need to be studied in order, according to some definite system," he wrote, "but simplicity should prevail—simplicity of arrangement and simplicity of language." Thus, Boothe set out to write a succinct and accessible theological handbook.[2]

WHO WAS CHARLES OCTAVIUS BOOTHE?

On June 13, 1845 Charles Octavius Boothe was born in Mobile County Alabama. He was the legal property of Nathaniel Howard.

As a slave he was treated relatively mildly. "I think I can say that [my master] and I really loved each other," he wrote.[3] Nevertheless, he was a frank critic of slavery. He indicted all white Americans for imposing barbarous

1. Edward R. Crowther, "Charles Octavius Boothe: An Alabama Apostle of 'Uplift,'" *The Journal of Negro History* 78, no. 2 (1993), 113.

2. Charles Octavius Boothe, *Plain Theology for Plain People* (Philadelphia: American Baptist Publication Society, 1890), 11.

3. Charles Octavius Boothe, *The Cyclopedia of the Colored Baptists of Alabama: Their Leaders and Their Work* (Birmingham: Alabama Publishing Company, 1895), 10.

conditions upon his people.[4] Proponents of slavery argued that God used the practice to bring blacks to salvation; in contrast, Boothe contended that the gospel spread to slaves *despite* chains and oppression. "As for you, you meant evil against me; but God meant it for good, to bring it about that many people should be kept alive, as they are today." (Gen 50:20 ESV). God takes no pleasure in the denial of his image; yet nothing prevents his will.[5]

Nearly four million slaves were freed by the Emancipation Proclamation in 1865. Still, blacks remained captive to social and economic norms that complicated daily life. Legislation did not eradicate four hundred years of white contempt. Former slaves had few skills, resources, and institutions to support themselves. Due to these economic challenges, sharecropping—freed slaves rented and tended part of a white farmer's land in exchange for a variable percentage of its yield—became a common practice for blacks. They still lacked the means to be truly independent.

Racial uplift was Boothe's consuming passion. Following the Civil War (1861–1865), he worked to improve the spiritual, social, and intellectual well-being of blacks in a society that denied their humanity before God and in its Constitution.[6] Boothe focused on education because an educated black populace contradicted the notion among whites that blacks would regress into "savagery."[7]

Boothe learned how to read at a young age. At the age of three he learned the alphabet from the lettering of a tin plate. His ability was nurtured by several teachers who boarded at the estate where he was enslaved.

As a teenager, Boothe worked as a clerk at a local law firm. He explored Scripture on a regular basis, because mid-nineteenth-century legal practice was rooted in biblical logic. As he became increasingly conversant with the Bible, his faith matured. From childhood he prayed and heard the Bible read, but Boothe said that "In 1865 ... I reached an experience of grace which so strengthened me as to fix me on the side of God's people."[8] In March of 1866 he received baptism.

---

4. Crowther, "An Alabama Apostle of 'Uplift,'" 111.

5. Boothe, *Cyclopedia of the Colored Baptists of Alabama*, 20.

6. Crowther, "An Alabama Apostle of 'Uplift,'" 112. See U.S. Const. art. I, § 2.

7. William Van Deburg, *Slavery and Race in American Popular Culture* (Madison: University of Wisconsin Press, 1984), 123.

8. Boothe, *Cyclopedia of the Colored Baptists of Alabama*, 10.

For Boothe the church must play a crucial role in racial uplift. He established and pastored two churches: First Colored Baptist Church in Meridian, Mississippi, and Dexter Avenue Baptist Church in Montgomery, Alabama. Dexter Avenue Baptist Church was always a pillar in the Montgomery community, but in recent decades, it has become internationally renowned for its role in the Civil Rights Movement under the leadership of its twentieth pastor, Martin Luther King, Jr. (1929-1968). It has been renamed King Memorial Baptist Church.

In the years following Emancipation, the church became the epicenter of the black community. The church was the sole institution that African Americans controlled, and it was central to the black community—not only as a spiritual outpost, but also as a social hub and political nerve center. Often the most educated people in the black community were pastors who had the rhetorical skill necessary to advocate for their congregants. Moreover, full-time ministers at large churches were uniquely situated to advocate for racial justice. They were financially independent from whites, so they could represent blacks on social issues without fear of lost wages—though they could suffer other forms of retaliation like church burning, physical violence, and intimidation.

Ordained ministers like Boothe played a significant role in elevating literacy rates among black Southerners from 10 percent in 1860 to nearly 43 percent in 1890.[9] Boothe promoted literacy so former slaves could read the Bible and break free of the oppressive interpretive practices that made the Christian faith a tool to subjugate blacks during slavery. By reading the Bible for themselves blacks could escape manipulative interpretations that were used to foster docility in slaves and make obedience to their masters synonymous with obedience to God.

He engaged society based on the biblical premise that all people are granted equal dignity as divine image bearers. Boothe's theological convictions compelled him to be vocal concerning immigration.[10] In 1901 he joined

---

9. Eric Foner, *Reconstruction: American's Unfinished Revolution, 1863-1877* (New York: Harper & Row, 1988), 96.

10. Crowther, "An Alabama Apostle of 'Uplift,'" 114.

Booker T. Washington (1856–1915) to oppose Alabama's legal disenfranchisement of blacks.[11]

Boothe established institutions vital for blacks to flourish beyond slavery's chains. He taught for the Freedmen's Bureau, which supported black education and provided emancipated slaves food, shelter, medical care, and legal assistance. As a member of the Colored Baptist Missionary Convention, Boothe facilitated literacy programs and theological training for black preachers and laypeople. In 1878 he and other convention leaders founded Selma University; he served as its second president (1901–1902). Boothe also served as the editor of *The Baptist Pioneer*, which helped underwrite Selma University.

In his life and ministry Boothe emphasized interracial cooperation—even though he ministered during the onset of Jim Crow Segregation and at the height of lynching terror—perhaps in part because as a boy Boothe had had positive interactions with whites. At a Baptist church near his home, whites and blacks worshiped together, served each other, and washed each other's feet. Whites and blacks alike sought out his grandmother, a respected woman of prayer, for comfort during times of sorrow.[12] So he cooperated with those willing to support black social advancement and combat racial oppression despite their race. Boothe worked collaboratively with white Baptist groups like the Alabama Baptist Convention (of the Southern Baptist Convention), the American Baptist Home Missionary Society, and philanthropists to obtain funding for training ministers and for the operating expenses of Selma University.[13]

After decades of pastoral ministry, educational innovation, and public engagement, Boothe doubted the effectiveness of his efforts for racial reconciliation in the South. The pace of change was slow. In 1910—just before the Great Migration (1915–1930), when 1.6 million blacks moved from the rural South to Midwestern and Southern cities—Boothe moved to Detroit, where he died in 1924. Little is known of his time in Detroit—not even the precise date of his death.

---

11. See Booker T. Washington, "Petition to the Members of the Alabama Constitutional Convention," in *Booker T. Washington Papers Volume 6: 1901–2*, ed. Barbara S. Kraft (Champaign: University of Illinois, 1977), 129–33.

12. Boothe, *Cyclopedia of the Colored Baptists of Alabama*, 9.

13. Crowther, "Charles Octavius Boothe."

WHY REVIVE *PLAIN THEOLOGY FOR PLAIN PEOPLE?*

Plain Theology for Plain People *destroys reductionist stereotypes of black faith.* Many are unfamiliar with the African American theological heritage because of its limited corpus. Black Christianity is largely an oral tradition, and its written resources have been obscured by racial bias. Today, as in Boothe's time, many tend to caricature black Christian faith as merely "religious feeling and fervor."[14]

Plain Theology for Plain People *shows black evangelicals that they belong in the broad evangelical tradition.* Many thoughtful black Christians—often educated in evangelical universities and seminaries—have an enduring sense of homelessness in the evangelical tradition. Their ancestors are seldom, if ever, included as contributors to Evangelicalism. Boothe offers a window into an underexplored vista of theological expression. Black evangelicals have equal claim to the evangelical tradition—even though evangelicals have historically muted their voice.

Plain Theology for Plain People *requires evangelicals to engage non-white theological voices.* Because evangelical biblical and theological studies have excluded the voices of racial minorities, evangelical theology is shaped by the concerns of the dominant culture. Unfortunately, white evangelicals only hear minority evangelicals' theology if it echoes white evangelical voices.

Unity in Christ demands an openness to collaboration and to mutual sharpening in the theological task. Evangelicals often presume that the task of theology is merely to comprehend God. But the goal of theology is wisdom—a lived demonstration of knowing God. God, not context, has ultimate authority, and yet wisdom demands understanding the context in which Christians live and God works.

Christians need Christians from different cultural, historical, and socioeconomic contexts to develop wisdom. Boothe grappled with God's relation to late-nineteenth-century black life—including economic disenfranchisement, lynching terror, and legal segregation. Chronological and cultural distance allows readers today to see how Boothe embodied divine wisdom

---

14. W. E. B. DuBois, "Of the Faith of the Fathers," *The Souls of Black Folk* (Chicago: A. C. McClurg, 1903), 197.

in his context. As a result, believers are encouraged by God's actions in the past: the Lord God is faithful in every circumstance.

Plain Theology for Plain People *exemplifies how the Bible informs Christian doctrine*. Systematic theologians continually fight the temptation to conform Scripture to a theological system (be it Reformed Theology, Liberation Theology, or Neo-Orthodox Theology). While every theological paradigm ought to be based on Scripture, not every verse fits neatly into a system. With his audience in mind, Boothe reinforces the sufficiency of Scripture by giving an organized account of how Scripture informs Christian doctrine. Through his biblical centrality Boothe circumvents the theological skirmishes of the academy. Like Boothe, theologians today must make the lofty ideas of theology plain to common Christians.

WORKS CITED

Boothe, Charles Octavius. *Plain Theology for Plain People*. Philadelphia: American Baptist Publication Society, 1890.

———. *The Cyclopedia of the Colored Baptists of Alabama: Their Leaders and Their Work*. Birmingham: Alabama Publishing Company, 1895.

Crowther, Edward R. "Charles Octavius Boothe: An Alabama Apostle of 'Uplift.'" *The Journal of Negro History* 78, no. 2 (1993): 110–16.

———. "Charles Octavius Boothe." *The Encyclopedia of Alabama*. June 3, 2008; http://www.encyclopediaofalabama.org/article/h-1560.

DuBois, W. E. B. "Of the Faith of the Fathers." *The Souls of Black Folk*, 189–206. Chicago: A. C. McClurg, 1903.

Foner, Eric. *Reconstruction: American's Unfinished Revolution, 1863–1877*. New York: Harper & Row, 1988.

Van Deburg, William. *Slavery and Race in American Popular Culture*. Madison: University of Wisconsin Press, 1984.

Washington, Booker T. "Petition to the Members of the Alabama Constitutional Convention." In *Booker T. Washington Papers Volume 6: 1901–2*, edited by Barbara S. Kraft, 129–33. Champaign: University of Illinois Press, 1977.

*To the memory of the late devoted
Rev. Harry Woodsmall, of Indiana.
A consecrated Christian gentleman; a faithful teacher of the
word of God; a self-sacrificing friend of the Lord's poor; a
man whose life was a living illustration of the divine life of
the Bible; a man, the memory of whose labors for the colored
people of the South must be as unfading as the eternities to
come, and as lasting as the immortality of the souls who wear
his impress, is this little book lovingly dedicated by the author.*

– *Preface*

The writer of this little volume has been influenced to attempt its production by special circumstances, involving peculiar needs. Very early in life he was led to the study of the Holy Scriptures and to the exercise of a personal and saving faith in their Author. While yet but a child he was assured of a divine call to the office of the gospel ministry, for the duties of which office he had no means of preparation. Having no instructor, he sought to inform himself by means of books, the Bible being his chief reliance.

The progress made in systematic knowledge of holy things—as might have been expected—was very slow and exceedingly tedious. He needed a work on Systematic Theology. At last he began to meet with such works, but as their authors wrote in the midst of educational surroundings, their style was far above his comprehension. Hence the advance he made was still slow and tedious. But in time, in the absence of a person better qualified, he came to the position of instructor of Ministers' and Deacons' Institutes, in which it was necessary to discuss the doctrines of the Bible after something like a regular system. The men were unlearned, and hence the system needed to be especially simple. The works extant all supposed some educational attainments in their readers. Therefore, though at this time the books on theology were useful to him, they gave but little direct assistance to his pupils. An independent course, taking in the forms of thought and modes of expression peculiar to the people, was attempted as the only means to the desired end. Of course, it was then expected that the need for such a special plan would soon pass away, when the plan itself would necessarily cease. But as the necessity has continued the plan has continued also. And even now circumstances call, not for the discontinuance of the special system, but for its perfection and extension. The doctrines of our holy religion need to be studied in order, according to some definite system; but simplicity should prevail—simplicity of arrangement and simplicity of language.

This plea for plainness is made because of these facts: 1. The great masses of mankind are still unlearned, still unaccustomed to the rules of logic, to long processes of reasoning, while they know nothing of the mysteries of science. 2. Leadership—natural leadership—is often born in the hovels of the poor and the homes of the uneducated. 3. The private members of churches who have but little time for books, but have great need for the truths that books teach, should find the truth suited to their time, their understanding, and their wants. Indeed, our hope lies in the religious education of the whole people.

These remarks are by no means intended as criticisms upon theologians or upon the theological works extant. All the writer means to say is this: There are people who live on a plain so far beneath the mental heights of these works as to be unable to reach up to them and enjoy their spiritual blessings. For these people there come to us calls for the preparation of special works—calls which, in the name of Christ, we must try to answer.

The writer would therefore remind the reader that this little book's only mission is to help *plain* people in the study of the *first* principles of divine truth. Critical examinations and exhaustive discussions do not fall within the purpose of this work. Hence, trusting that its purpose may be understood by the learned, and praying to God to give it acceptance in the hearts of the earnest and simple minded, the author respectfully submits the humble production to the candid judgment of his fellow men.

1

Being and Character of God

The knowledge of God and of the divine government is sometimes called the science of theology. If this be so, it is the science of all sciences. God is first, then come his works. Man is made to obtain knowledge; Solomon says: "Also, that the soul be without knowledge, it is not good" (Proverbs 19:2).

When ignorant, a man is helpless, defenseless; he knows not what to do nor which way to go; and what knowledge can avail more to our security, peace, honor, and prosperity than that knowledge which acquaints us with the character of our Creator, Saviour, Preserver, and Judge, and instructs us in those laws which determine our relations in life and fix our hopes for eternity?

Before the charge "know thyself," ought to come the far greater charge, "know thy God." But, though the study of the being and character of God is a duty which we dare not disregard, still, let us not be unmindful of the fact that we vile, short-sighted worms should approach the solemn task of studying God with feelings of humility and awe. God is found of the lowly, but hides himself from the proud and self-sufficient man. When Daniel fasted and prayed and made confession of sin, the secrets of the Lord were unfolded to his view.

Let us consider:

I. WHERE GOD APPEARS TO US

(1) IN THE WORKS OF CREATION

"The heavens declare the glory of God, and the firmament showeth his handi-work. Day unto day uttereth speech, and night unto night showeth knowledge" (Psalm 19:1-2).

"The invisible things of him [of God], from the creation of the world are clearly seen, being understood by the things that are made, even his eternal power and Godhead" (Romans 1:20).

When we look upon the heavens and the earth, fashioned by almighty power, and guided by the excellency of wisdom, we see with our eyes and handle with our hands the evidence of the existence and personality of a superior Being.

Man has met no being greater than himself, and he knows that the starry hosts, the mountains, the seas, and the living creatures around him, are not the workmanship of his skill and power: he knows they did not come from his hands. Then who did make these things? That they came from a Being infinitely greater than man is plain, from the fact that the works of creation infinitely excel anything in the works of man. A human track in a desert would be to me conclusive evidence that a human foot had trodden that desert. Thus Paul argues that the things which are seen and handled are proofs of the unseen things.

We have never seen a thought, nor a purpose, nor an emotion; yet we know that there are thoughts, purposes, and emotions, by what we can see and hear; even the words and deeds which thoughts and purposes create. It is thus that we see God in creation.

(2) IN THE WORKS OF PROVIDENCE (GENESIS 9)

"Who in times past suffered all nations to walk in their own ways; neverthe-less he left not himself without witness, in that he did good, and gave us rain from heaven, and fruitful seasons, filling our hearts with food and gladness" (Acts 14:16, 17).

In the fall of 1889, Henry M. Stanley, writing to the *New York Herald*, says, with reference to his most eventful African expedition: "A veritable divinity seems to have hedged us as we journeyed. I say it with all reverence. It has impelled us whither it would, effected its own will, but nevertheless guided and protected us .... I endeavored to steer my course as direct as possible, but there was an unaccountable influence at the helm." The vulgar will call it luck, unbelievers will call it chance, but deep down in each heart there remains the feeling that in verity there are more things in heaven and earth than are dreamed of in common philosophy. I refer to this experience and confession of Stanley, not because of the novelty or oddity of the experience, but because of the boldness of the confession. For whether we are manly enough to confess it or not, we all, at times, feel with Shakespeare—

"There is a divinity that shapes our ends,
    Rough-hew them how we will."

Let it not be forgotten that I am contending that there is such a thing as a general as well as a special providence; there is the supervision of the works of creation, especially of the intelligent creation.

Where is the philosopher who can declare and explain the laws by which the winds and clouds are forced to beat to the fields and springs a full and regular supply of dew and rain? They seem to be subject to freaks, and yet for thousands of years they have been held to the line as with bit and bridle, and so have been the carriers of life, beauty, and gladness to plant, to beast, to man. The following paragraph is taken from an article by Dr. Townsend, published in a number of the "Golden Rule," in the year 1889, and is worthy of note, because it shows that the masses of mankind perceive in nature that God is there: in other words, it shows that the human mind is possessed of the idea of the presence of God in the works of nature:

"The leading thought to which we call attention is this, that the human mind is in possession of the idea that there is something in the universe that properly may be called a Supreme Being. The proof of this is beyond reasonable question. The testimony, for instance, of Aristotle, is of weight. 'By the primitive and very ancient men,' he says, 'it has been handed down in the form of myths, and thus left to later generations, that it is the Divine which holds together all nature.'

"The words too of Plutarch are equally weighty: 'If we traverse the world, it is possible to find cities without walls, without letters, without kings, without wealth, without coin, without schools and theatres; but a city without a temple, or that practiceth not worship, prayer, and the like, no one ever saw.' And says Dr. Livingstone, speaking of the then newly discovered tribes of the interior of Africa, 'They have clear ideas of the Supreme God.' Different names have been used, but all peoples have had the idea of some kind of a God or Supreme Being. The early Chinese called this Being the 'One God'; the Northmen called him the 'Invisible Odin'; the North American Indians called him the 'Great Spirit'; the ancient Peruvians called him the 'Sun God'; the Persians called him the 'Source of Light'; the people of India called him 'Brahm'; Plato called him the 'All'; the Greeks called him 'Zeus'; the Romans called him 'Jupiter'; the Mussulmans called him 'Allah'; the Jews called him Jehovah, and most civilized nations of the present time call him God.

"It always has been and it is now difficult to find any person who is an out and out atheist [or a no-God man]. It is admitted that now and then a man is met who says, 'I don't believe in a God.' But such a man is usually very superstitious, and when exposed to danger or death he will be found praying for help. Professor Tyndall, in his Belfast address, speaking of the strength of this God idea, says:

"'No atheistic reasoning can, I hold, dislodge religion from the heart of man; logic cannot deprive us of life, and religion is life to the religious; as an experience of the consciousness, it is perfectly beyond the assaults of logic.'

"'Faith in a God,' says Lichtenberg, 'is instinct. It is natural to men, just as going on two legs is natural. With many it is modified, and with many it is stifled; yet it exists, and is indispensable to the (internal) symmetry of consciousness.'

"'Naturally as the new-born draws nourishment from its mother's breast,' says Jacobi, 'so the heart of man takes hold on God in surrounding nature.'

"Renan seemed for a while to be drifting into Atheism: but his words of late represent the feelings of many persons who belong to his class of thinking, and at least imply a personal God.

"'One thing only is certain,' he says: 'it is that the fatherly smile at certain hours shines across nature, and assures us that there is an eye looking at us, and a heart which follows us.'

"Such are the facts in support of the statement that the human mind is possessed with the idea of a Supreme Being."

See Nehemiah 9:6; Psalms 36:6; 2 Chronicles 16:9; 2 Corinthians 4:17.

(3) In the Holy Scriptures

(a) In the harmony of the records with the voice of nature.

Of the works of creation they simply say:

"In the beginning God created the heavens and the earth" (Genesis 1:1).

Speaking of the providence to which I have alluded, they say:

"While the earth remaineth, seed time and harvest, cold and heat, and summer and winter, and day and night, shall not cease" (Genesis 8:22).

Agreeing with the experience of Stanley and all other men who have lived with their eyes open, it is written:

"O Lord, I know that the way of man is not in himself: it is not in man that walketh to direct his steps" (Jeremiah 10:23; see Proverbs 16:1, 9; 19:21).

"Man's goings are of the Lord" (Proverbs 20:24; see Daniel 2:20-23; 1 and 2 Kings).

(b) In its moral law in Exodus 20:1-17, and Deuteronomy 5:1-21. The head and socket at the knee joint, and the tongue and groove in the ceiling do not fit each other so closely and so neatly as this law fits the needs of the human heart. And the world could have day without the light of the sun as easily as man could have life and blessedness without the observance of these commandments. This law demands that men shall worship God and love one another, neither of which principles have origin in the depraved nature of man. Hence the source of this law, like the works of creation, starts higher than the mind of man, and declares the presence of a heart that is pure and holy.

(c) In its prediction of future events.

When some who were carried away captives to Babylon seemed to be hopeful of a speedy return to their own land, Jeremiah sent word to them to build them houses, for they were consigned to captivity for seventy years—to the time of the overthrow of Babylon, at which time they should be allowed to return to their homes.

"Build ye houses, and dwell in them; and plant gardens and eat the fruit of them;

"Take ye wives, and beget sons and daughters; and take wives for your sons, and give your daughters to husbands, that they may bear sons and daughters; that ye may be increased there, and not diminished.

"And seek the peace of the city whither I have caused you to be carried away captives, and pray unto the Lord for it: for in the peace thereof shall ye have peace.

"For thus saith the Lord of hosts, the God of Israel; let not your prophets and your diviners, that *be* in the midst of you, deceive you, neither hearken to your dreams which ye cause to be dreamed.

"For they prophesy falsely unto you in my name: I have not sent them, saith the Lord.

"For thus saith the Lord, That after seventy years be accomplished at Babylon I will visit you, and perform my good word toward you, in causing you to return to this place" (Jeremiah 29:5-10; see, also, 25:12).

Seventy years pass by and we come to the following record of the proclamation of Cyrus:

"Now in the first year of Cyrus king of Persia, that the word of the Lord by the mouth of Jeremiah might be fulfilled, the Lord stirred up the spirit of Cyrus king of Persia, that he made a proclamation throughout all his kingdom, and put it also in writing, saying:

"Thus saith Cyrus king of Persia, The Lord God of heaven hath given me all the kingdoms of the earth; and he hath charged me to build him a house at Jerusalem, which *is* in Judah.

"Who *is there* among you of all his people? his God be with him, and let him go up to Jerusalem, which is in Judah, and build the house of the Lord God of Israel (he *is* the God), which *is* in Jerusalem.

"And whosoever remaineth in any place where he sojourneth, let the men of his place help him with silver, and with gold, and with goods, and with beasts, besides the freewill offering for the house of God which *is* in Jerusalem" (Ezra 1:1-4; see Daniel 9:22-24).

Compare the following with the present state of Babylon:

"And Babylon, the glory of kingdoms, the beauty of the Chaldees' excellency, shall be as when God overthrew Sodom and Gomorrah.

"It shall never be inhabited, neither shall it be dwelt in from generation to generation: neither shall the Arabian pitch tent there; neither shall the shepherds make their fold there.

"But wild beasts of the desert shall lie there; and their houses shall be full of doleful creatures; and owls shall dwell there, and satyrs shall dance there.

"And the wild beasts of the islands shall cry in their desolate houses and dragons in *their* pleasant palaces: and her time *is* near to come, and her days shall not be prolonged" (Isaiah 13:19-22).

But here is a declaration of future events covering many hundreds of years. Nothing can be more certain evidence of the presence of a divine mind than the uncovering of times and things and seasons yet to come, especially when these stretch over a great many years. Passing over much very interesting testimony as to the signs of God's presence in the Bible, I come to what to me seems to be the crowning testimony; namely, the *Messianic idea*. Whoever traces the development of this Christ-thought in the Bible, from Genesis 3:15, through all its forms, down to the manger at Bethlehem, and thence to the cross, through the tomb, and on to the ascension—whoever traces this idea, with humble purpose to be informed, must of necessity perceive that it is but the unfolding of an eternal purpose, involving not only all of man's earthly history and mortal career, but having in view his interests in the world to come. Nor can he fail to see that the incidents which were to attend upon the development of the idea were all under the eye of him from whom the purpose came. See Chapter Third on "The Way of Salvation." The works of creation, the operations of providence, and the Sacred Scriptures clearly show the presence of a Being of infinite power, infinite knowledge, infinite wisdom, and perfect excellence of character; and where these attributes appear, there the presence of God is declared.

II. WHAT MAY BE KNOWN OF HIM

(1) "God is a Spirit" (John 4:24)

The great truth that meets us at the beginning of our study of the divine nature is that God is not akin to matter, that he is not akin to those things which may be seen with the eyes, heard with the ears, and handled with hands. He is Mind, Spirit; not manifesting himself in weight, measure, figure, etc., but manifesting himself in qualities and activities, in powers, in knowledge, in wisdom, in disposition. We get an idea of the Biblical view of the spirit-nature from the words of Jesus to his frightened disciples:

"Behold my hands and my feet, that it is I, myself; handle me and see; for a spirit hath not flesh and bones as ye see me have" (Luke 24:39).

From this expression, it would seem that the Master meant by these words that even if the spirit might assume form so as to be seen, or might assume voice so as to be heard, yet certainly it could not have flesh and bones, as he had. Perhaps man, in all things, tends to grow into the features of his surroundings. The man who has never seen other homes and other countries is apt to think that other homes and other countries are like his own. He is also likely to think that spirits must be somewhat like bodies, that God's existence is like the existence of men. God teaches us to guard against this idea in the command:

"Thou shalt not make unto thee any graven image, or any likeness of any thing that is in heaven above, or that is in the earth beneath, or that is in the water under the earth" (Exodus 20:4).

Moses, as he rehearses the law to the children of Israel, says:

"Take ye therefore good heed unto yourselves (for ye saw no manner of similitude on the day that the Lord spake unto you in Horeb out of the midst of the fire); lest ye corrupt yourselves and make you a graven image, the similitude of any figure" (Deuteronomy 4:15, 16).

We have not a single word in the history of Eden which denotes that Adam and Eve ever saw any form of God. It is said that they heard the *voice* of the Lord God walking in the garden in the cool of the day. Indeed, the whole tenor of the Bible is one continuous lesson, teaching men that they must not attempt to make to themselves any image of God, or to worship him in figures and forms. Said Jesus to the woman at the well:

"God is a spirit, and they that worship him must worship him in spirit and in truth" (John 4:24).

As the creature-life is one of matter and forms, it is hard for us to understand a higher order of life—a life that has no body and that needs no forms. However, we perceive dimly the truth that God is a spirit, and believe it, waiting for eternity to bring us more light. That there are spiritual essences, we know; for we have perceived the existence of thought, to which we have never attached the ideas of weight, measure, form, or color.

(2) GOD IS SELF-EXISTENT

When God ordered Moses to return to Egypt on his mission of deliverance to Israel, Moses desired to know by what name he preferred to be presented to Israel. God replied:

"I AM THAT I AM. ... thus shalt thou say unto the children of Israel, I AM hath sent me unto you" (Exodus 3:14).

After Moses had begun his work of deliverance, and at a time when his faith is sorely tried, God says to him:

"I appeared unto Abraham, unto Isaac, and unto Jacob by the name of God Almighty, but by my name Jehovah was I not known to them" (Exodus 6:3).

This word Jehovah, evidently, is intended to give the same meaning as the expression, "I AM THAT I AM." And this is the same as to say: "My name is the Living, Eternal, Immutable One." Such a Being would present a glorious contrast with the dying, momentary, changeable forms of created life about those to whom the name was spoken. We cannot duly appreciate self-existence till we consider the forms of life and motion which appear in the creature. That power by which the clock points its hands to the passing hours is not in the clock; it came out of the brain and hand of its maker and of him that winds it up. That power with which the steam engine draws its forty or fifty cars comes not out of the engine, but out of the mind of the machinist and from the heat of the flame in its bowels. Man's life comes not of himself: it comes from the Living God, the Fountain of Life; it is sustained by his food, his drink, and the air round about him. About every four seconds he must drink in the air, in order to keep his little spark of life aglow. His life is not in himself. Not so with God. The sources of life are all in him. "The Father hath life in himself" (John 5:26). "In him [the Son also] was life" (John 1:4). The works of creation are witnesses of these Scripture declarations, as may be seen in the following thoughts: 1. God made the universe, or the universe made itself; that would mean, nothing made something. 2. If God made the universe, he was before the universe. 3. If he could live when there was nothing but himself, it is plain that he can live without any being or creature but himself. 4. He cannot live independent of other things, except the causes of life are in himself; for if the life were in other things, those things might be cut off from him and leave him lifeless. The glory of this doctrine of the self-existence of God Almighty is enhanced as we meditate upon the multiform and manifold life possessed by him. No wonder it is said: "Who is like unto thee, O Lord?"

(3) God is eternal

"Lord, thou hast been our dwellingplace in all generations. Before the mountains were brought forth, or ever thou hadst formed the earth and the world, even from everlasting to everlasting, thou art God" (Psalm 90:1, 2).

"Before the hills in order stood,
     Or earth received her frame,
   From everlasting thou art God,
      To endless years the same."

Here again we mortal worms come up to the brink and look into the deeps of mystery to see nothing but mystery. We look at the gray-headed sire, wearing the marks of fourscore years and ten; upon the great trees, which have withstood the storms and tempests of centuries; upon the mossy rocks, which were washed by the rains that fell before the days of Enoch; upon the sun, and the moon, and the stars, which for thousands on thousands of years have marched the pathless ways of the heavens, sentinels on the watchtower of eternity. We count millions, millions, millions back, back, back into the ages gone by, and we are still in the midst of the life of God. Thus, having exhausted our feeble strength trying to look into the past eternity, we have no power to do more than turn our eyes upon the future, and exclaim: *"He is, ever has been and ever shall be!"*

Now, the possibility of this attribute is found in his self-existence, omnipotence, sovereignty, and wisdom. Why may not a being who is life itself have eternity of existence? That which dies does so because it cannot continue to live. Whatever God wills, that shall come to pass.

(4) HE IS OMNIPRESENT—EVERYWHERE

"Whither shall I go from thy spirit? or whither shall I flee from thy presence? If I ascend up into heaven, thou art there: if I make my bed in hell, behold thou art there. If I take the wings of the morning and dwell in the uttermost parts of the sea, even there shall thy hand lead me, and thy right hand shall hold me. If I say, Surely the darkness shall cover me: even the night shall be light about me" (Psalm 139:7-11).

"Am I a God at hand ... and not a God far off? Do not I fill heaven and earth?" (Jeremiah 23:23, 24; see Jonah 1).

The omnipresence of God appears in the activities of nature, it appears in the supervisions of providence, it appears in the voice of conscience, and it appears in the conquests of righteousness. Even the desert waste has some signs of order in it; while the poor heathen fears and trembles under a sense that there is a God who sees his actions, and who will bring him into judgment for the same.

(5) God is omniscient—has all knowledge

"Hell and destruction are before the Lord: how much more then, the hearts of the children of men? The eyes of the Lord are in every place, beholding the evil and the good" (Proverbs 15:11, 3).

"Can any hide himself in secret places that I shall not see him? saith the Lord" (Jeremiah 23:24).

"Neither is there any creature that is not manifest in his sight; but all things are naked and opened unto the eyes of him with whom we have to do" (Hebrews 4:13).

Jonah goes into the bottom of the ship, but God sees him. Elijah goes into the cave of the mountain, far away in the desert, but ere long there falls upon his ear, "Elijah, what doest thou here?" Before him hell has no covering and the future has no secrets.

> *"Oh, wondrous knowledge, deep and high!*
> *Where shall a creature hide?"*

Who is the man that has sinned, and then has not felt that he was pursued by the eye of God? Where is the sinner who has not desired to ease and to relieve his heart from the piercing, accusing gaze of the eye of the Judge?

"I am God, and there is none like me, declaring the end from the beginning, and from ancient times the things that are not yet done" (Isaiah 46:9, 10).

As the parts of a watch lie open before the eye of its maker, so all things that he has made lie opened before the eye of God.

> *"How careful then ought we to live!*
> *With what religious care!"*

(6) God is omnipotent

The infinite power of God is manifest—

(a) In Creation.

"In the beginning God created the heavens and the earth" (Genesis 1:1).

Let us suppose ourselves to be occupying a point somewhere in space, and to be conscious of the absence of all forms of matter, of all sorts of force, and of all mental, moral, and spiritual activities—no world, no air, no life, no spirit. Suppose that while we are wondering at the silent waste around us, we hear a voice, saying, "Let hosts of suns be, and let planets, revolving about them, come forth; on these planets let the dry land be broken with seas and rivers; let the waters be filled with fishes and great ocean monsters; let there be winged fowl to fly in the air in the open firmament; and trees, and grasses, and creeping things, and four-footed creatures to live upon the dry land." Suppose these things, and then suppose that while the voice is yet speaking, it is being done before our eyes. We see the suns bursting forth into flaming worlds and their several planets taking their places in order around. We see the plant, the fish, the creeping thing, the fowl, the beast, each after his kind, appearing in his time. But we see no being of mind and conscience like ourselves. As we begin to feel a little lonely and desirous of society with our kind, we hear the same voice, saying, "Let a being of intellectual and moral qualities appear in the flesh." As the words are spoken a creature like ourselves stands before us. We commune with him and are assured that he is really a copy of ourselves. Would we want more evidence than this to prove Almighty power?

(b) In the Government of Creation and in Providence.

For ages on ages these wondrous works have moved on in harmony with the divine will. Each world has kept its own path, and each living creature has multiplied after his kind, the seas have kept their bounds, the winds and clouds have brought the rain and dews on time, and in spite of all the brutalizing and demoralizing agencies that the world and Satan have put forth against man, he is still above the brute, and still aspiring to the society of God. Not least, the lion's jaws are locked, and the heated furnace cannot burn against his will.

(c) It appears in God's control of men and demons in the interest of his moral government. Nebuchadnezzar, the king of Babylon, was compelled to say:

"Blessed be the God of Shadrach, Meshach, and Abednego, who hath sent his angel and delivered his servants that trusted in him and have changed the king's word" (Daniel 3:28).

When the king after this grew proud, God drove him from his throne and from among men till he was humbled, and said:

"Now I, Nebuchadnezzar, praise and extol and honour the God of heaven, all whose works are truth and his ways righteousness" (Daniel 4:37).

(Read the whole of the book of Daniel.)

"Ask of me and I will give thee the heathen for thine inheritance and the uttermost parts of the earth for thy possession" (Psalm 2:8; Daniel 7:13, 14; Psalm 33:6, 9, 11).

"O Lord God of hosts, who is a strong Lord like unto thee?" (Psalm 89:8).

(7) GOD IS ALL-WISE

"Oh, the depth of the riches both of the wisdom and knowledge of God!" (Romans 11:33).

With the late devoted Harry Woodsmall, the term wisdom was a favorite word, and his life illustrated its meaning. As the twelve golden "settings" in the breastplate of Judgment (spoken of in Exodus 28), bore the twelve precious stones set in them, so a broad and clear conception, of the end of life, had arranged and fixed the place of every sort of knowledge in his possession, in such a way that all he knew naturally contributed to the honor of Christ. The different items of our knowledge may be likened unto the precious stones that are to be set in the breastplate referred to. Wisdom consists in the ability to apply the various items of our knowledge, in such a way as to accomplish a desired end, and may be likened to the ability to arrange the precious stones each in its proper place. Of course, this attempt to symbolize must not be carried too far. Yet we have seen men with a large amount of information who, from a lack of wisdom, were not able to arrange, adjust, and crystallize what they knew into a life of beauty and usefulness. Then we have seen others with wisdom for the proper setting of precious stones, but no beautiful stones of knowledge to place in the breastplate. The wisdom of God is manifest in his choice of the ends that he purposes to accomplish, and in the selection of the means to secure these ends. This wisdom is apparent:

(a) In the designs and adaptations of nature.

(b) In the dispensations of providence.

(c) In the purposes and plans of grace. It is a contemplation of wisdom in the works of grace that excites Paul to exclaim:

"How unsearchable are his judgments, and his ways past finding out" (Romans 11:33).

(8) GOD IS INFINITELY HOLY AND PERFECTLY JUST

(a) Holiness.

"I saw also the Lord sitting upon a throne, high and lifted up, and his train filled the temple. About it stood the seraphim: each one had six wings; with twain he covered his face, with twain he covered his feet, and with twain he did fly. And one cried unto another and said, Holy, holy, holy is the Lord of hosts" (Isaiah 6:1-3).

"And they rest not day and night, saying, Holy, holy, holy is the Lord God Almighty, which was, and is, and is to come" (Revelation 4:8).

"Who is like unto thee, O Lord, among the gods? who is like unto thee, glorious in holiness, fearful in praises, doing wonders?" (Exodus 15:11).

These exhibitions, or pictures of the Divine Being, are sublime and awful. As the brightness of the noonday sun causes the stars to cover themselves in paleness, so the brightness of God's awful moral excellence causes these heavenly creatures to veil their faces and hide their feet beneath their wings ere they speak of the glory which they see. The perfect holiness of God is seen in the rectitude of the divine character; it is the sum of all supreme, moral excellence. Holiness is said to be glorious (Exodus 15:11), and reference is made to the beauty of holiness (1 Chronicles 16:29; 2 Chronicles 20:21; Psalm 29:2).

(b) Justice.

While holiness is the rectitude of the divine character, justice is the rectitude of the divine government. It means equal laws in righteous execution for the government of God's intelligent creatures. We need not remind the reader that it is plain that nothing other than a just or righteous government could possibly originate or exist in such lofty, moral perfection as is seen in the character of God. Can perfect holiness and infinite wisdom give birth to unrighteous laws and unequal administrations?

"The Lord is righteous in all his ways and holy in all his works" (Psalm 145:17).

"Judgment will I also lay to the line, and righteousness to the plummet" (Isaiah 28:17).

That we may be duly impressed with this awful attribute of our God, let us consider it a little further. Like the Being of whom it is a quality, it is unchangeable and eternal. God's judgments are always righteous. This makes their fearful aspect to the man or angel who dares to transgress his law, which is holy and just and good. The wicked it punishes, but the righteous it rewards. It spares none who are found on the side of sin—no, not even the sinless Christ, when he graciously appeared in the sinner's place.

"And if my soul were sent to hell,
    Thy righteous law approves it well."

(9) He is true and faithful

"Thy word is truth" (John 17:17).

"Ascribe ye greatness unto our God. He is a Rock, his work is perfect: for all his ways are judgment: a God of truth and without iniquity is he" (Deuteronomy 32:3, 4).

"The Lord is the true God" (Jeremiah 10:10).

"For all the promises of God in him are yea, and in him Amen" (2 Corinthians 1:20).

As Joshua drew near to death, he called the elders of Israel about him, and said:

"I am going the way of all the earth; and ye know in all your hearts and in all your souls, that not one thing hath failed of all the good things which the Lord your God spake concerning you; all are come to pass unto you, and not one thing hath failed thereof" (Joshua 23:14). Compare Genesis 8:22–9:17 with Acts 14:17, and with what we have seen on the line of the Scriptures here referred to.

God has been true and faithful to his law; thousands of years ago, he declared that life and prosperity would come of obedience, and that ruin and death would come of sin. It is true before our eyes, and ever has been true. He promised deliverance and mercy to the penitent: deliverance and mercy comes to the penitent. He promised to give us a Saviour: the Saviour has been given, and now the world is full of the sounds of his salvation. See 2 Thessalonians 1:7–9. That which is fulfilled assures the fulfillment of what remains in promise.

"Hath he spoken, and shall he not make it good?" (Numbers 23:19).

(10) God is immutable, unchangeable

"Of old hast thou laid the foundations of the earth: and the heavens are the work of thy hands. They shall perish, but thou shalt endure: yea, all of them shall wax old like a garment; as a vesture shalt thou change them, and they shall be changed: but thou art the same, and thy years shall have no end" (Psalm 102:25–27).

"I am the Lord, I change not" (Malachi 3:6).

"Every good gift and every perfect gift is from above, and cometh down from the Father of lights, with whom is no variableness, neither shadow of turning" (James 1:17).

"God is not a man that he should lie; neither the son of man that he should repent" (Numbers 23:19).

We foolish, erring creatures are filled with uncertainty, vacillations, changes; but these come of our imperfections. We need knowledge, wisdom, and holiness. Change belongs to man, not to God, who is perfect. A being who alters his purposes, or is fickle in his plans, is not perfect—is not perfect in intellect nor perfect in character. And it is declared: "He is a Rock; his work is perfect." But leave off all other evidence, and the immutability of the moral law is proof of the unchangeableness of God. That which was true was righteous in the days of Adam and Moses and Daniel, is still true and right, and ever shall be so; and justice calls as loudly for vengeance now as it called in the days of Cain.

(11) HE IS GOOD AND MERCIFUL. GOODNESS AND MERCY APPEAR—

(a) In the works of creation.

"And God saw everything that he had made; and behold it was very good" (Genesis 1:31).

"And out of the ground made the Lord God to grow every tree that is pleasant to the sight and good for food; and the tree of life also in the midst of the garden" (Genesis 2:9).

"And the Lord God said, It is not good that man should be alone; I will make him a help meet for him" (Genesis 2:18).

Nothing is more plainly written in creation than the evidence that God is disposed to fill his creatures with happiness. He has given us eyes to see, and has spread around us beautiful things to be seen. He has created sweet sounds, and given us ears to hear them. He has filled the world with good things, and given us power to enjoy them.

(b) In his providence.

"He maketh his sun to rise on the evil and on the good, and sendeth rain on the just and on the unjust" (Matthew 5:45).

"The Lord is gracious and full of compassion, slow to anger, and of great mercy. The Lord is good to all: and his tender mercies are over all his works" (Psalm 145:8, 9).

How tender are those words which the angel Gabriel bore to Daniel the prophet:

"O Daniel, a man greatly beloved!" (Daniel 10:11; Acts 14:17).

(c) Especially in the work of redemption.

"God so loved the world that he gave his only begotten Son, that whosoever believeth in him should not perish, but have eternal life" (John 3:16).

God *so* loved the world, *so* loved us, his enemies, that God made this matchless, amazing sacrifice to open to us again the gates of life!

"He that spared not his own Son, but delivered him up for us all, how shall he not with him also freely give us all things?" (Romans 8:32).

"Behold what manner of love the Father hath bestowed upon us that we should be called the sons of God" (1 John 3:1).

"God is love," is the Soul of kindness. Hitherto we may have trembled, as we gazed upon the awful majesty of Jehovah, but here we draw nigh with hope; for where goodness, mercy, and love are found, there the poor, helpless, heart-sick, repentant sinner may secure a hearing, and hope to find grace to help in times of distress and need.

III. THE UNITY OF GOD

"Hear, O Israel: The Lord our God is one Lord!" (Deuteronomy 6:4).

"One God and Father of all, who is above all, through all, and in you all" (Ephesians 4:6).

God is one essence, one character, one mind; not many essences, not many minds. These different attributes are not different gods, but different qualities of the same God, and exist in and are of the same essence.

Different moral conditions call for different exhibitions of the divine character. For example, on wicked Sodom justice rains down fire and brimstone, while for the children of Israel in the wilderness, goodness and mercy supply a daily table with bread from heaven for the space of forty years. Omnipotence divides the sea for the deliverance of the Hebrews; and, then and there, in the warm tracks of mercy, the floods return to the destruction of the Egyptian hosts. Two nations are camped by the side of the Red Sea. God is between the hosts. Out from him goes forth the day upon one camp; and out from him goes forth the midnight darkness upon the other (Exodus 14). At one time God saves a people whom he afterward destroyed. To the ignorant and superstitious, these things would naturally suggest the idea of many gods, or of many independent parts in the same God. Out of the first idea would come many different images; out of the last idea would come an image of many faces. Hence the need of the lesson on the unity of God. His nature, his character, his purposes are one. Closing this short chapter, I would remind the reader that nature is witness that there is but one God. If we look only about the earth, upon the changing seasons and shifting clouds, it may seem to us that there are opposing forces in the elements of nature; but if we lift our eyes above the confusions of earth till they come into view of the heavenly bodies—the sun, moon, and stars—we must see that the universe, in which our world is only a little speck, is arranged in the most glorious order. No signs of opposing wills or of clashing powers are there.

In the earth there is evidence that there is but one God. We see it in the fact that all creatures multiply after their kind. It is especially apparent in the divine law, which law is one and the same law in all parts of the world and in all ages (Psalm 86:10; Isaiah 44:8; John 17:3).

"I am the Lord, and there is none else; there is no God besides me" (Isaiah 45:5).

The fearful consequences of disobedience at this point are seen in Romans 1:20-32.

IV. THE TRINITY

Here I speak with rather more fear than usual, and yet I speak; for the holy book has spoken before me. The doctrine declared here is that God, who is one in substance and one in character, exists in three persons, the Father, the Son, and the Holy Spirit.

I would observe that this doctrine is revealed to us in the Sacred Scriptures.

Some writers have thought that there is a reference to the Trinity in the words which precede the account of the creation of man:

"And God said, Let us make man in our image, after our likeness" (Genesis 1:26).

They think that the words "us" and "our" imply that there are different persons in the Godhead, who are more distinctly revealed afterward; others, however, do not think that the use of these words furnishes any definite proof of the existence of the Trinity.

It is not necessary to rest the proof of the doctrine on any doubtful passage. In the New Testament the doctrine is presented in such a peculiar manner as to establish it on a firm foundation.

"And Jesus, when he was baptized, went up straightway out of the water: and ... he saw the Spirit of God, descending like a dove ... and lo, a voice from heaven, saying, This is my beloved Son, in whom I am well pleased" (Matthew 3:16, 17).

"Go ye, therefore, and teach all nations, baptizing them in the name of the Father, and of the Son, and of the Holy Ghost" (Matthew 28:19).

At the river Jordan, God the Son is represented as rising from the water, the Spirit appears in the shape of a dove, and lights upon him, while the voice of the Father proclaims the Son and expresses his pleasure in him. In the Great Commission, the names of the Spirit and Son are put in equal honor with the name of the Father. This forever forbids our speaking of the Holy Spirit as a "mere influence," or of the Son as being inferior to the Father.

"But when the Comforter is come, whom I will send unto you from the Father, even the Spirit of truth, which proceedeth from the Father, he shall testify of me" (John 16:26).

"The grace of the Lord Jesus Christ, and the love of God, and the communion of the Holy Ghost be with you all" (2 Corinthians 13:14).

"Through him [the Son] we both have access by one Spirit unto the Father" (Ephesians 2:18; John 14:17, 26; 16:7–15).

No doctrine of the Christian faith is more plainly taught than that there are three persons in the Godhead. We cannot comprehend it, but we can accept it as the truth, and wonder, worship, and wait for the time in which we shall know as we are known.

Let us think of the Godhead in a trinity of persons, the majesty of his Being, and the glory of his works; think of this happy, eternal, almighty, and glorious companionship! The sublimity and majesty of the thought is overwhelming! As I dwell upon this sight, the thought arises in my mind that, at some point in the past eternities, God said, "Let us bring forth creatures in our likeness, that they too, for our glory, may be happy in the blessedness of our exalted fellowship." And at this point, ere the morning stars began their first notes of praise, the purposes of grace were formed and decreed, "so it seems good in thy sight" (Matthew 11:25). Proverbs 8:22–30 is a ray of light bursting out from the mysteries of this divine companionship:

"The Lord possessed me in the beginning of his way, before his works of old. I was set up from everlasting, from the beginning, or ever the earth was ... When he prepared the heavens, I was there: when he set a compass upon the face of the depth: when he established the clouds above: when he strengthened the fountains of the deep: when he gave to the sea his decree that the waters should not pass his commandment: when he appointed the foundations of the earth: then I was by him as one brought up with him: I was daily his delight, rejoicing always before him."

In Jesus' last prayer, we look in upon this companionship from another side:

"O Father, glorify thou me with thine own self, with the glory which I had with thee before the world was" (John 17:5, 24).

In this council Christ was slain (in purpose) from before the foundation of the world (Revelation 13:8). In the work of redemption, the Persons of the Trinity seem to occupy different offices. The Father sends the Son, who restores the law; and the Son sends the Spirit, who restores the life.

"As thou hast sent me into the world, even so have I also sent them into the world" (John 17:18; 20:21; Isaiah 9:6).

"When he had by himself purged our sins, sat down on the right hand of the Majesty on high" (Hebrews 1:3).

"But the Comforter, which is the Holy Ghost, whom the Father will send in my name, he shall teach you all things, and bring all things unto your remembrance, whatsoever I have said unto you" (John 14:26).

"If I go not away, the Comforter will not come unto you; but if I depart I will send him" (John 16:7; see John 3:8).

But the operations of the different offices so beautifully and so perfectly agree in character and aim as to be the most conclusive evidence before us of the unity and equality of these Divine Persons in one glorious Godhead.

— CHAPTER

2

Man

I. HIS CREATION

"And God said, Let us make man in our image, after our likeness: and let him have dominion over the fish of the sea, and over the fowl of the air, and over the cattle, and over all the earth, and over every creeping thing that creepeth upon the earth. So God created man in his own image, in the image of God created he him."

"And the Lord God formed man of the dust of the ground and breathed into his nostrils the breath of life; and man became a living soul" (Genesis 1:26, 27; 2:7).

There are important facts in his creation.

(1) MAN DOES NOT APPEAR UPON THE STAGE OF ACTION TILL THE EARTH HAS BEEN COMPLETED FOR HIS RECEPTION, TILL "GOD SAW THAT IT WAS GOOD."

Before the "lord" of the earth appears his habitation is prepared to receive him (Genesis 1:25).

(2) MAN'S NATURE.

Though his body was made from the dust of the ground, still his true being, his higher nature, was a spiritual essence, after the nature of God. No other than a spiritual essence or nature is capable of receiving a moral impress, or of attaining unto the relation of citizenship in the divine government. Moral image and moral obligations suppose a spiritual being.

(3) God made man upright, and a holy disposition, like that of God—in whose mind he was conceived—was freely given unto him.

In view of these facts, it is easy to see the purpose of man's creation. Why was all this careful preparation, except for a great and important purpose? Man was created in the image of God, in order that he might be fit for the presence of God, and prepared to enjoy fellowship with him and with other holy beings whom he had created. But man was, in knowledge, an infant, and, in position, a subject of him who had created him.

II. MAN MADE SUBJECT TO SPECIAL GOVERNMENT

When God placed him in the garden prepared for his habitation, he laid upon him the command:

"Of the tree of the knowledge of good and evil, thou shalt not eat of it: for in the day thou eatest thereof, thou shalt surely die" (Genesis 2:17).

It was with God as it is with parents when an infant comes into the family. With the child there are two stages of discipline. The first stage belongs to that period in which the child cannot, for the want of development, discern the virtue of principle. At this point we teach him to regard parental authority by giving him special commands, often giving no reasons except that such is our choice. Then comes the period when we appeal to principles and laws, and drill by them. But no matter what the season, obedience to the parental will and regard for authority must be maintained. This necessity existed in the case of our first parents. They must be taught, and must understand, that God himself is law. The tree is called "the tree of the knowledge of good and evil," and it is said of it that its fruit was good for food and pleasant to the eyes. It had in itself, it appears, no extra virtue; it was a peculiar tree only because it was guarded by a peculiar command from God. God must needs begin at some point to teach and to enforce his authority upon Adam, and he chooses to begin with the command in regard to this one tree.

"Of all the trees of the garden, except *this one,* thou mayest freely eat."

Here God put the bridle of restraint upon man, but let the reins drop so that man might hold them himself. It appears that for some time he went on well under the discipline imposed upon him. He not only kept up with the work of "keeping and dressing" the garden, but he kept clear of all meddling with the one specially forbidden tree. How we could wish that he had continued obedient until by discipline he had become perfected and established in righteousness!

I know that no sane man will contend that God should not have put man under command. Some one may ask why God left Adam. To this I reply that the only act that has any personal virtue in it is the act that is born of the intelligent, deliberate, obedient choice of the actor; and the act that is performed only because of the presence of another has in it no virtuous character at all.

III. THE PENALTY OF TRANSGRESSION

"In the day thou eatest thereof thou shalt surely die" (Genesis 2:17).

In other words: "In the day thou breakest across the command which I set before thee, thou shalt lose thy life." Let us look into the facts in the case and we shall see the beauty of the truth before us.

Man was a being who had two natures, we may say; he was an animal from the elements of the ground; he was also a spirit, a being of mental and moral powers, fitting him to study and treasure up the facts of knowledge and to the principles of law. It is very evident that the spirit is the higher part of man's nature; that is, is *the man*, for the reason that nothing but a spirit can possess and regard moral relations to the divine government. Hence the words "Thou shalt lose thy life" were spoken especially of the spiritual nature. By referring to Genesis 2:7, we may see what is the life of the soul:

"And the Lord God formed man of the dust of the ground and breathed into his nostrils the breath of life; and man became a living soul."

Here we are told that the breath of God made man a *living* soul—a *living* soul, in contradistinction from a *dead* soul. If nothing save the breath of God in man can make him a living soul, it is plain that the absence of this breath of life must leave him dead, even though no wrath from God should be added.

God, the Righteous Judge of the universe, cannot permit and encourage disobedience in his creatures by filling their hearts with his life and blessings. Indeed, they who willfully disobey God, of necessity separate themselves from him and invite upon their heads God's holy displeasure against rebels and rebellion. Nature is not a contradiction of herself—how much less so is nature's God. Right is right, and wrong is wrong, and the one can never and can nowhere be the other. To leave God is not to be with him, and he only is the Life, as well as the Father of spirits.

IV. MAN FELL OF HIS OWN CHOICE

"And when the woman saw that the tree was good for food, and that it was pleasant to the eyes, and a tree to be desired to make one wise; she took of the fruit thereof, and did eat; and gave also unto her husband with her, and he did eat. ...

"And they heard the voice of the Lord God walking in the garden in the cool of the day: and Adam and his wife hid themselves among the trees of the garden. And the Lord God called unto Adam and said unto him, Where art thou? And he said, I heard thy voice in the garden: and I was afraid because I was naked and I hid myself" (Genesis 3:6, 8-10).

This third chapter gives the history of the fall. It tells of the cunning of Satan, who, presenting himself in the person of the serpent, professed special concern for man's improvement; he wanted that they should rise from their slavish, ignorant condition to "be as gods, knowing good from evil."

Speaking to the woman, he says:

"Ye shall not surely die: for God doth know that in the day ye eat thereof, then your eyes shall be opened, and ye shall be as gods, knowing good and evil" (Genesis 3:4, 5).

Thus he hints that God is deceiving them, and keeping them from their highest good. Instead of resisting the devil, Eve gave him respectful attention, loosed her faith from about the word of the Lord, put her confidence in his enemy, disobeyed the command, and ruined her soul. Here, some one may ask, why God did not exclude the tempter, forbidding his presence in the garden.

I do not know why he did not, but we all know this: A friend who cannot remain true to a friend in the presence of his friend's enemy is unworthy the name of friend; and the character that cannot stand except when it is imprisoned and guarded is without virtue: it is only a sham.

Moreover: As the sunshine and storms deepen the roots and toughen the trunk of the tree, so trials and temptations should fix our principles and deepen our convictions. Can we have any guarantee of character, any proof of moral excellence, where there have been no temptations to test our genuine worth? All things are proven before they are sealed. Silver and gold are refined by the wash and the furnace, and are proven by the tests.

To this one thought I turn special attention; namely, Eve's fall began within her, in her thoughts and feelings, before her fall was made known by outward act. There were but three steps from life into death. The first step was to doubt the word of the Lord; the second step was to believe the word of the devil; and the last step was to eat the fruit. She took these steps in quick succession, and landed in hopeless despair. There is but one unlocked "trapdoor" to hell, and that is unbelief in the true God. Eve and Adam fell through this door. All who have fallen in all ages have fallen through this door. This still is the direct route to the "outer darkness where there is wailing and gnashing of teeth."

(1) Immediate results of the Fall

Obedience was their covering, their righteousness, their robe of heavenly citizenship. While this remained untorn they were honorable, appearing in royal apparel. But now it is torn, and their nakedness shames them. They are troubled for garments, and fall to "sewing fig leaves together" to cover themselves. These dry and crumble and fall off. God is heard. They flee from his approaching voice, and seek to hide among the thick trees of the garden. He pursues them, overtakes them, holds them to trial. For the first time, that lordly pair of creatures begin to experience complainings and bitter feelings against each other. Here we come in sight of the first signs of human cowardice and deception. The man lays the blame on the woman, and the woman lays it on the serpent. Here it may be asked why God did not perfect their faith in him, so that doubt would have been impossible. Replying to this, I would say that active faith is composed of two operations; namely, first, it is the putting forth of evidence on one side, and, second, it is the acceptance of this evidence on the other. In the case of faith in God, it engages two parties: First, God puts forth the word which he wants us to receive. He shows us the strength of that word. What remains to be done must be done by us; that is to say, man must perform the part of resting on the word put before him. God put the word before Adam; he satisfied Adam of his power, wisdom, sovereignty, and goodness. God had done his part. Now if Adam refused to rest his confidence, his interests, and hopes in him, it is plain that the fault was entirely his own.

"Therefore the Lord God sent him forth from the garden of Eden, to till the ground from whence he was taken. So he drove the man out: and he placed at the east of the garden of Eden Cherubim and a flaming sword, which turned every way, to keep the way of the tree of life" (Genesis 3:23, 24).

Sad sight! Bitter cup! Dark and doleful future! The soul is leprous! Woe to the world for the mournful sounds and woeful sights which it must now hear and see!

(2) MORAL EFFECTS UPON THE RACE

We need not go far to see how Adam's sin has affected his offspring. Look at those blood stains on the hands of Adam's oldest son. Those stains come not from the slaying of the beast: it is the blood of his brother Abel, whom he slew in the fields. Cain is no exception.

"All we like sheep have gone astray; we have turned every one to his own way" (Isaiah 53:6).

"The Lord looked down from heaven upon the children of men, to see if there were any that did understand and seek God. They are all gone aside, they are all together become filthy: there is none that doeth good, no, not one" (Psalm 14:1, 2).

"By one man's disobedience many were made sinners" (Romans 5:19).

"The heart is deceitful above all things, and desperately wicked" (Jeremiah 17:9).

That one act of disobedience plunged the world in sin and misery.

"By one man sin entered into the world and death by sin; and so death passed upon all men" (Romans 5:12).

"By the offence of one, judgment came upon all men to condemnation" (Romans 5:18).

Sin of every name, and disease of every form, come upon his seed through his crime. But we are not coerced sinners; for each man is a sinner in his own will, a sinner of his own choice.

"The righteousness of the righteous shall be upon him, and the wickedness of the wicked shall be upon him" (Ezekiel 18:20).

(3) LEGAL EFFECTS UPON THE RACE

"The soul that sinneth, it shall die" (Ezekiel 18:20).

A beautiful thought is this:

"The Lord God breathed into his nostrils the breath of life, and man become a living soul" (Genesis 2:7).

Is it not intended by this expression to signify God's nearness to man? Two must be close together, when the one can breathe into the nostrils of the other. Is it not a hint to man that he must keep his life-receiving apparatus close to the mouth of God, if he would be a living soul? But sin parts a man from God: it is a departure from him and a straying far away.

Then sin deserves to be punished. Sin is a tremendous and fearful evil. What it has done is proof of this. No man ever sinned and failed to feel its ill desert. Its horrors and ruin are in itself. How can God let it go unpunished? So it is written:

"The wrath of God is revealed from heaven against all ungodliness and unrighteousness of men" (Romans 1:18).

"There is no respect of persons with God. As many as have sinned without law shall perish without law; and as many as have sinned in the law shall be judged by the law" (Romans 2:11, 12; Ephesians 2:1–3).

Alas! without God in this world, and without hope for the world to come (Ephesians 2:12). No hope, no help, no plea, no audience with the King, no friend, no advocate with God—lost, lost, lost! Desolation and death reign!

3

The Way of Salvation

I. THE PURPOSE OF GRACE ORIGINATED WITH GOD

"For God so loved the world, that he gave his only begotten Son, that whosoever believeth in him should not perish, but have everlasting life" (John 3:16).

This is the language of the Son of God, and is a wonderfully compact statement of the way of salvation from the mighty and gracious Saviour himself. It does not state when the purpose was formed; but there are many passages in the Scriptures which show that it was no afterthought in the mind of God. The first indication of the purpose of God to save sinners is found in immediate connection with the sad story of the Fall. In the Garden of Eden both the justice and the mercy of God are manifested. Justice demands that the sinners should be driven from the Garden; but before the Lord God compels them to go he graciously sets a star of hope in their dark skies. He speaks to the serpent in a way to arouse anxious fear in his mind, and at the same time to allay the fear of Adam and Eve. He says:

"Because thou hast done this ... I will put enmity between thee and the woman, and between thy seed and her seed; it shall bruise thy head, and thou shalt bruise his heel" (Genesis 3:14, 15).

Then also God showed his kind care for the guilty man and his wife, for we read that before they are driven forth—

"Unto Adam also and his wife did the Lord God make coats of skin and clothed them" (Genesis 3:21).

What a touching picture passes before our minds as we read this short, but pathetic record! God is thus hiding the shame of their nakedness, but he is doing it at the sacrifice of life; for their coats are made of the skins of slain beasts. Is there a hint that their lives are to be saved by the death of another? Every action suggests the idea of previous preparation on the part of God to meet this sad emergency.

But along with this indirect testimony the Scriptures give us, for the strengthening of our faith and hope, plain and positive statements.

"Blessed *be* the God and Father of our Lord Jesus Christ, who hath blessed us with all spiritual blessings in heavenly *places* in Christ:

"Accordingly as he hath chosen us in him before the foundation of the world, that we should be holy and without blame before him in love:

"Having predestinated us unto the adoption of children by Jesus Christ to himself, according to the good pleasure of his will.

"To the praise of the glory of his grace, wherein he hath made us accepted in the beloved:

"In whom we have redemption through his blood, the forgiveness of sins, according to the riches of his grace:

"Wherein he hath abounded toward us in all wisdom and prudence;

"Having made known unto us the mystery of his will, according to his good pleasure which he hath purposed in himself" (Ephesians 1:3–9).

"Forasmuch as ye know that ye were not redeemed with corruptible things, *as* silver and gold, from your vain conversation *received* by tradition from your fathers;

"But with the precious blood of Christ, as of a lamb without blemish and without spot:

"Who verily was foreordained before the foundation of the world, but was manifest in these last times for you" (1 Peter 1:18–20).

"Who hath saved us, and called *us* with a holy calling, not according to our works, but according to his own purpose and grace, which was given us in Christ Jesus before the world began" (2 Timothy 1:9).

"And all that dwell upon the earth shall worship him, whose names are not written in the book of life of the Lamb slain from the foundation of the world" (Revelation 13:8).

"From the foundation of the world." The use of this expressive phrase is worthy of special note. Dr. Justin A. Smith, in his "Commentary on Revelation," 13:8, says that this "is the New Testament mode of representing what took place in the remote past, before time, as measured in the periods of this world, had existence." The phrase would be properly translated in most cases, "from eternity." It has this meaning undoubtedly in the words of our Lord's prayer, "Thou lovedst me before the foundation of the world" (John 17:24).

II. THE PURPOSE OF GRACE HAD ITS ORIGIN IN THE LOVE OF GOD

It is well to consider the love of God that prompted the purpose of saving men from the fearful consequences of their own disobedience. Of course, it was not the kind of love with which he regarded Jesus Christ. There could have been nothing in the character of man so pleasing to God as that which shone forth in him of whom the Father said:

"This is my beloved Son, in whom I am well pleased" (Matthew 3:17).

It was not what has been called "the love of complacency." It was a love that combined pity for those who were in a very pitiable condition, and a desire to do them good by raising them out of it and establishing them in a better and happier state. It was what is termed "the love of compassion." It was a truly wonderful love; the more we think of the sinfulness of sin, the more wonderful the love of God will appear to us. We naturally ask, "Why did God so love sinners?" and the only answer that we can give is, "Even so, Father, for so it seemed good in thy sight." Well may we exclaim with the beloved disciple:

"Behold what manner of love the Father hath bestowed upon us, that we should be called the sons of God" (1 John 3:1).

"In this was manifested the love of God toward us, because that God sent his only begotten Son into the world, that we might live through him. Herein is love, not that we loved God, but that he loved us, and sent his Son to be the propitiation for our sins. Beloved, if God so loved us, we ought also to love one another" (1 John 4:9–11).

III. THE GREATNESS OF THE GIFT OF GOD

"He gave his only begotten Son." When the gracious purpose of God was formed there was, of course, present to the divine mind the vastness of the work of redemption; and there was need to select those means and agencies that could bring full salvation to sinners, and at the same time make manifest the justice, the wisdom, the grace, and the love of God. It was a marvelous work that was to be accomplished. To all the holy angels that surround the throne of God, and to the innumerable company of the redeemed, it will be the subject of devout meditation through all the everlasting ages of heaven.

When short-sighted and imperfect men have a work of vast importance to be accomplished, they need to weigh with the utmost care the means to be employed, in order that the plan selected may meet every necessity of the case. But we must not imagine that God is altogether such an one as ourselves. All things are fully opened before his all-seeing eyes. When he in his infinite wisdom adopts a plan, that plan, like his law which the Psalmist so highly extols, is holy and just and good. "The law of the Lord is perfect" (Psalm 19:7). Thus perfect is the plan of salvation.

The plan which infinite love and wisdom adopted involved the *giving* of his only begotten Son as the Saviour of men; it also involved the necessity that his well-beloved Son should do what the apostle says he subsequently did:

"Made himself of no reputation, and took upon him the form of a servant, and was made in the likeness of men:

"And being found in fashion as a man, he humbled himself, and became obedient unto death, even the death of the cross" (Philippians 2:7, 8).

The giving was not a mere sending; it was therefore not a mere mission in which he was made of no reputation, but it also included as an essential part that he should humble himself and become obedient unto death, even the agonizing and shameful death of the cross. God gave, or sacrificed, his well-beloved Son to such humiliation, such agony, such a death.

Since Jesus Christ was the God-man, having the divine nature of the Son of God united to the human nature of the Son of David, he was able to become sin for us, to bear up our sins in his own body on the tree (1 Peter 2:24), to suffer in his human nature as he could not suffer as the Son of God; while his nature as the Son of God gave a value and efficiency to his suffering which it would not and could not have had in a merely human nature.

IV. FOR WHOM THE SALVATION OF GOD WAS PREPARED

The words of our Lord give us definite information on this subject:

"And as Moses lifted up the serpent in the wilderness, even so must the Son of man be lifted up:

"That whosoever believeth in him should not perish, but have eternal life.

"For God so loved the world, that he gave his only begotten Son, that whosoever believeth in him should not perish, but have everlasting life" (John 3:14–16).

These words tell us the purpose of God in the preparation of a way of salvation. It was the actual salvation of them that believe in God's only begotten Son. This is manifest from the words "whosoever believeth," which are so wide in meaning as to include all believers everywhere in all the world, through all generations, even until the end of the world shall come. The emphatic words of the Lord Jesus on the mountain of Galilee also hear decided testimony to the gracious import of the purpose of God. As he stood there after his resurrection, and near to the time of his ascension to heaven, his thoughts went out toward all at that time dwelling on all the surface of the earth, and onward through all the centuries, even until the end of the world. With all of these multitudes present to his mind, he laid the solemn injunction on his disciples, saying:

"All power is given unto me in heaven and in earth.

"Go ye therefore, and teach all nations, baptizing them in the name of the Father, and of the Son, and of the Holy Ghost:

"Teaching them to observe all things whatsoever I have commanded you: and, lo, I am with you always, *even* unto the end of the world. Amen" (Matthew 28:19, 20).

"And he said unto them, Go ye into all the world, and preach the gospel to every creature.

"He that believeth and is baptized shall be saved; but he that believeth not shall be damned" (Mark 16:15, 16).

It is evident from these words that every person in all the world, down to the end of time, needs the salvation that God has provided, and that no one who really desires to be made a partaker of its blessings shall ever be turned empty away.

There are two classes of persons, that differ in some respects, though essentially alike. One of these classes is composed of such as are lulled into a false security by the supposition that they have always tried to do their duty to their fellow-men, and never have done anything that is very bad. They go on their way to meet the solemn judgment of God, saying, "Peace, peace; when there is no peace" (Jeremiah 6:14). They perish at last, because they have not believed on the Son of God. Those belonging to the other class have been aroused for a time to some just sense of their sin and danger, but are wont to say that they have been such desperate and determined sinners, they have sinned in such various ways and so deeply, that there can be no salvation for them. They never go to the Lord Jesus, and, like the self-righteous class, they also perish, because they have not believed on the Son of God.

These two classes, so seemingly different, are alike in one very important respect. They both have a deep and settled conviction that salvation is to be procured by their own works. But the gospel of God teaches that there is no salvation, and can be no salvation, for a sinner by his own works, but only by the one means that God has appointed; that is, by faith in the only begotten Son of God. The Apostle Paul has put this truth in a very clear, positive, and impressive form:

"We *who are* Jews by nature, and not sinners of the Gentiles. Knowing that a man is not justified by the works of the law, but by the faith of Jesus Christ, even we have believed in Jesus Christ, that we might be justified by the faith of Christ, and not by the works of the law: for by the works of the law shall no flesh be justified" (Galatians 2:15, 16).

Those, therefore, that wish to be instrumental in leading sinners to Christ should make special efforts to impress on their minds first the solemn truth, that without the salvation that God has provided they must inevitably perish. The strongly emphatic words of the apostle should be pointed out to them, and they should be earnestly exhorted to meditate earnestly upon them until their sad meaning has been clearly comprehended.

"We have before proved both Jews and Gentiles, that they are all under sin; as it is written, There is none righteous, no, not one; there is none that understandeth, there is none that seeketh after God. They are all gone out of the way, they are together become unprofitable; there is none that doeth good, no, not one" (Romans 3:9–12).

In view of this universal sinfulness and utter ruin of men, the Lord has made the following statements, which certainly can give no comfort to the self-righteous, or to those who for any reason are neglecting the great salvation; but give all necessary encouragement to those who feel their need of God's salvation, and desire to become partakers of its blessings.

"If ye believe not that I am he, ye shall die in your sins" (John 8:24).

"They that are whole have no need of the physician, but they that are sick: I came not to call the righteous, but sinners to repentance" (Mark 2:17).

V. THE DOOM FROM WHICH BELIEVERS ARE SAVED

This fearful doom is set forth in the one comprehensive word, "perish." It means, in the case of a sinner, the end of everything that can make existence desirable. It is total and final separation from God, the source and fountain of all true blessedness; the cessation of all those pleasing anticipations that have been wont to throw their brightness on the future toward which men are always advancing; the end of all those hopes that have been to them strength in weakness, help in difficulties, comfort in sorrows, and have made endurable long and weary hours of suffering. It makes the heart sink to think of that perdition which sweeps men away from all that is bright and cheery, and leaves them no prospect to the future but what has been graphically described as the blackness of darkness forever. How infinitely precious the salvation that delivers men from such a dark and terrible doom!

But there is still another blessing that should always be the occasion for deep thankfulness. In the announcement of the approaching birth of Jesus, the angel of the Lord said to Joseph:

"Thou shalt call his name Jesus, for he shall save his people from their sins" (Matthew 1:21).

The Apostle John also, in the Revelation, gives expression to the feeling that will always be found to be strong in the heart of the redeemed, in this world and the next:

"Unto him that hath loved us, and washed us from our sins in his own blood; and hath made us kings and priests unto God and his Father; to him be glory and dominion for ever and ever" (Revelation 1:5, 6).

It is the sin within man that debases, defiles; that is and always must be, a cause of wretchedness and woe. To be left forever, with all the love of sin and hatred of holiness and enmity to God that belong to the carnal heart, working within—that is a bottomless pit of utter misery. That is what it is to perish. What gratitude that the heart of man has ever felt; what thankfulness that the tongue of man has ever uttered, can express all that is due to God for salvation from such an awful perdition?

VI. THE BLESSINGS OF SALVATION

(1) IT BRINGS A SALVATION FROM SINS.

That is, it saves from sins themselves, as we have already seen; and it also secures a free pardon and deliverance from the penalties of sin.

"If we confess our sins, he is faithful and just to forgive us our sins, and to cleanse us from all unrighteousness" (1 John 1:9).

(2) IT BRINGS TO THE BELIEVER RECONCILIATION TO GOD.

"The carnal mind is enmity against God; for it is not subject to the law of God, neither indeed can be" (Romans 8:7).

It is not willing to submit to his authority, and is constantly refusing obedience to his law, which is holy and just and good. The Apostle Paul, however, who has so fully defined the intense enmity of the carnal mind to God, sets forth also the blessed results of God's great salvation in a very striking manner:

"And you, that were sometime alienated and enemies in your mind by wicked works, yet now hath he reconciled in the body of his flesh through death, to present you holy and unblameable and unreproveable in his sight" (Colossians 1:21, 22).

He does not refer here to the reconciliation of God to man. We cannot for a moment suppose that God, who so loved the world as to give his only begotten Son to such humiliation, suffering, and such a death, had any unwillingness to be reconciled to men. The change that was needed was a radical change in the mind of sinners. It is the Saviour that God was moved by his great love to give up to the task that was the means of reconciling them to God, making them to understand his grace, his goodnesss, his worthiness of their fullest confidence, and of that love which Jesus described when speaking of what the law required:

"Thou shalt love the Lord thy God with all thy heart, and with all thy soul, and with all thy mind, and with all thy strength: this is the first commandment" (Mark 12:30).

(3) IT BRINGS THE REDEEMED ONE INTO FELLOWSHIP WITH
THE FATHER, THE SON, AND THE HOLY SPIRIT; WITH
ALL THE HOLY ANGELS, AND THE MULTITUDE OF THE
RANSOMED SAINTS THAT SHALL ALL STAND IN SHINING
ROBES AROUND THE THRONE OF GOD IN HEAVEN.

(4) IT MAKES THE BELIEVER A PARTICIPANT IN THE ADOPTION
OF WHICH THE APOSTLE SPEAKS IN SUCH GLOWING TERMS:

"For as many as are led by the Spirit of God, they are the sons of God. For ye
have not received the spirit of bondage again to fear; but ye have received the
Spirit of adoption, whereby we cry, Abba, Father. The Spirit itself beareth
witness with our spirit, that we are the children of God: and if children, then
heirs; heirs of God, and joint heirs with Christ; if so be that we suffer with
him, that we may be also glorified together" (Romans 8:14-17).

4

The Son: His Coming and His Work

It has been said that the story of redemption begins with the love of God, in giving his only begotten Son, but that for all the details of the work of redemption, we need to study the history of the Son, beginning with his incarnation, extending through his life and work in this world, and his work as continued in heaven from the time of his ascension. That marked the end of his work in this world. He was appointed of God to his office as a Great High Priest, and having offered himself as a perfect sacrifice, we are told that he has entered "into heaven itself, now to appear in the presence of God for us" (Hebrews 9:24). No view of his work, therefore, can be complete that does not take into account that work.

(1) PROPHECIES OF HIS COMING

These prophecies go back to an early date, becoming more definite as the time for their fulfillment drew near.

"The sceptre shall not depart from Judah, nor a lawgiver from between his feet, until Shiloh come; and unto him *shall* the gathering of the people *be*" (Genesis 49:10).

"Therefore the Lord himself shall give you a *sign*: Behold, a virgin shall conceive, and bear a Son, and shall call his name Immanuel" (Isaiah 7:14).

"Seventy weeks are determined upon thy people and upon thy holy city, to finish the transgression, and to make an end of sins, and to make reconciliation for iniquity, and to bring in everlasting righteousness, and to seal up the vision and prophecy, and to anoint the Most Holy. Know therefore and understand, *that* from the going forth of the commandment to restore and to build Jerusalem, unto the Messiah the Prince, *shall be* seven weeks, and threescore and two weeks: the street shall be built again, and the wall, even in troublous times. And after threescore and two weeks shall Messiah be cut off, but not for himself: and the people of the prince that shall come shall destroy the city and the sanctuary; and the end thereof *shall be* with a flood, and unto the end of the war desolations are determined. And he shall confirm the covenant with many for one week: and in the midst of the week he shall cause the sacrifice and the oblation to cease, and for the overspreading of abominations he shall make *it* desolate, even until the consummation, and that determined shall be poured upon the desolate" (Daniel 9:24–27).

(2) HIS FORERUNNER

His forerunner's coming was foretold by Isaiah and Malachi some centuries before his appearance.

"The voice of him that crieth in the wilderness, Prepare ye the way of the Lord, make straight in the desert a highway for our God. Every valley shall be exalted, and every mountain and hill shall be made low: and the crooked shall be made straight, and the rough places plain: And the glory of the Lord shall be revealed, and all flesh shall see *it* together: for the mouth of the Lord hath spoken *it*" (Isaiah 11:3–5).

"Behold, I will send my messenger, and he shall prepare the way before me: and the Lord, whom ye seek, shall suddenly come to his temple, even the messenger of the covenant, whom ye delight in: behold, he shall come, saith the Lord of hosts. But who may abide the day of his coming? and who shall stand when he appeareth? for he *is* like a refiner's fire, and like fullers' soap: And he shall sit *as* a refiner and purifier of silver: and he shall purify the sons of Levi, and purge them as gold and silver, that they may offer unto the Lord an offering in righteousness. Then shall the offering of Judah and Jerusalem be pleasant unto the Lord, as in the days of old, and as in former years" (Malachi 3:1–4).

In the gospels we may read the narrative of the manner in which the promises of God were fulfilled.

"There was in the days of Herod, the king of Judea, a certain priest named Zacharias, of the course of Abia: and his wife *was* of the daughters of Aaron, and her name *was* Elisabeth. And there appeared unto him an angel of the Lord standing on the right side of the altar of incense. And when Zacharias saw *him*, he was troubled, and fear fell upon him. But the angel said unto him, Fear not, Zacharias: for thy prayer is heard; and thy wife Elisabeth shall bear thee a son, and thou shalt call his name John. And thou shalt have joy and gladness; and many shall rejoice at his birth. For he shall be great in the sight of the Lord, and shall drink neither wine nor strong drink; and he shall be filled with the Holy Ghost, even from his mother's womb. And many of the children of Israel shall he turn to the Lord their God. And he shall go before him in the spirit and power of Elias, to turn the hearts of the fathers to the children, and the disobedient to the wisdom of the just; to make ready a people prepared for the Lord" (Luke 1:5, 11–17).

"The beginning of the gospel of Jesus Christ, the Son of God; as it is written in the prophets, Behold, I send my messenger before thy face, which shall prepare thy way before thee. The voice of one crying in the wilderness, Prepare ye the way of the Lord, make his paths straight.

"John did baptize in the wilderness, and preach the baptism of repentance for the remission of sins. And there went out unto him all the land of Judea, and they of Jerusalem, and were all baptized of him in the river of Jordan, confessing their sins.

"And John was clothed with camel's hair, and with a girdle of a skin about his loins; and he did eat locusts and wild honey; and preached, saying, There cometh one mightier than I after me, the latchet of whose shoes I am not worthy to stoop down and unloose. I indeed have baptized you with water: but he shall baptize you with the Holy Ghost" (Mark 1:18).

The birth of John made an important era in the history of the Jewish people. It was promised, as is stated above, that his father, Zacharias, should "have joy and gladness," and also that "many shall rejoice at his birth"; and the reason for this was clearly stated, "for he shall be great in the sight of the Lord." All this was fulfilled. First, we read that his father had been smitten with dumbness, and remained speechless for several months, because of his slowness to believe what the angel said unto him; but on the eighth day after his birth the child was about to be circumcised, and by signs they asked his father what his name should be.

"And he asked for a writing table, and wrote, saying, His name is John. And they marvelled all. And his mouth was opened immediately, and his tongue *loosed*, and he spake, and praised God. And fear came on all that dwelt round about them: and all these sayings were noised abroad throughout all the hill country of Judea. And all they that heard *them* laid *them* up in their hearts, saying, What manner of child shall this be! And the hand of the Lord was with him.

"And his father Zacharias was filled with the Holy Ghost, and prophesied, saying, Blessed *be* the Lord God of Israel; for he hath visited and redeemed his people, and hath raised up a horn of salvation for us in the house of his servant David; as he spake by the mouth of his holy prophets, which have been since the world began" (Luke 1:63–70).

John did not enter for some years on his public ministry; but we read:

"And the child grew, and waxed strong in spirit, and was in the deserts till the day of his shewing unto Israel" (Luke 1:80).

When he was shown unto Israel, he became, as was foretold, eminently successful in his ministry.

The impression of his preaching was widely extended and very deep, as we see from the brief notices in the gospels. There was spread among the people, more widely than ever before, the expectation of a great Deliverer soon to appear; and there was also left on their minds the idea that he would not merely set up an earthly kingdom, but that the subjects of the coming Son of God must exhibit true repentance and be ready to forsake their sins. This was in so far a preparation for the teachings of the Lord. At the same time John's preaching roused deep hostility to himself on the part of many, who had no desire for God's salvation, just as did the preaching of Jesus when he began his work. It must not be forgotten, however, that John was only as the day star that heralded the coming of him who from the day of his appearing has been made manifest as "the Light of the world." John himself clearly understood his calling, for he said of him: "He must increase, but I must decrease" (John 3:30).

(3) THE INCARNATION

The slow but even development of the divine redemptive plan goes on, with increasing evidence of its vastness and wisdom, its grandness and glory. Like a dim lone star, it appears at first afar off; it moves up slowly, increasing in brightness, until, a blazing sun, it ascends into the zenith of the earth's dark sky. The long-promised Messiah comes; he comes at the time divinely appointed, he comes as "the Desire of all nations" (Haggai 2:7). In the whole history of the world there was no event of such vast importance as the

Incarnation of the Son of God. It had been prophesied that he should be born in Bethlehem of Judah:

"But thou, Bethlehem Ephratah, *though* thou be little among the thousands of Judah, *yet* out of thee shall he come forth unto me *that is* to be ruler in Israel; whose goings forth *have been* from of old, from everlasting" (Micah 5:2).

The fulfillment of this prophecy was brought about by a peculiar providence of God:

"And it came to pass in those days, that there went out a decree from Cesar Augustus, that all the world should be taxed. (*And* this taxing was first made when Cyrenius was governor of Syria.) And all went to be taxed, every one into his own city. And Joseph also went up from Galilee, out of the city of Nazareth, into Judea, unto the city of David, which is called Bethlehem; (because he was of the house and lineage of David:) to be taxed with Mary his espoused wife, being great with child. And so it was, that, while they were there, the days were accomplished that she should be delivered. And she brought forth her firstborn son, and wrapped him in swaddling clothes, and laid him in a manger; because there was no room for them in the inn" (Luke 2:1–7).

When the prophecy was fulfilled, the event was an occasion for rejoicing both in heaven and on earth. The sacred narrative informs us of these indications of lively interest and of grateful rejoicing:

"And there were in the same country shepherds abiding in the field, keeping watch over their flock by night. And, lo, the angel of the Lord came upon them, and the glory of the Lord shone round about them; and they were sore afraid. And the angel said unto them,

"Fear not: for, behold, I bring you good tidings of great joy, which shall be to all people. For unto you is born this day in the city of David a Saviour, which is Christ the Lord. And this *shall be* a *sign* unto you; Ye shall find the babe wrapped in swaddling clothes, lying in a manger.

"And suddenly there was with the angel a multitude of the heavenly host, praising God, and saying, Glory to God in the highest, and on earth peace, good will toward men. And it came to pass, as the angels were gone away from them into heaven, the shepherds said one to another, Let us now go even unto Bethlehem, and see this thing which is come to pass, which the Lord hath made known unto us. And they came with haste, and found Mary and Joseph, and the babe lying in a manger. And when they had seen *it*, they made known abroad the saying which was told them concerning this child.

"And all they that heard *it* wondered at those things which were told them by the shepherds. But Mary kept all these things, and pondered *them* in her heart" (Luke 2:8–19).

(4) THE MYSTERY OF THE INCARNATION

The statements of the Scriptures make clear to us that the Saviour that was to come is the Son of God.

"In the beginning was the Word, and the Word was with God, and the Word was God. The same was in the beginning with God. All things were made by him; and without him was not any thing made that was made. In him was life; and the life was the light of men.

"And the Word was made flesh, and dwelt among us, (and we beheld his glory, the glory as of the only begotten of the Father,) full of grace and truth" (John 1:1–4; 14).

"For verily he took not on *him the nature of* angels; but he took on *him* the seed of Abraham. Wherefore in all things it behooved him to be made like unto *his* brethren, that he might be a merciful and faithful high priest in things *pertaining* to God, to make reconciliation for the sins of the people" (Hebrews 2:16, 17).

We do not understand this mystery—that is, how the Son of God, the second person in the Blessed Trinity, took upon him the seed of Abraham, and was made in the likeness of men; but there are two things that we do understand: first, that a Being possessed of the divine nature and exhibiting superhuman excellences of mind and character has appeared in human nature; second, that such a Being was and still is the crying need and longing desire of mankind. We need an Immanuel, a "God-with-us." We needed a "day's man," a Mediator, one whose nature, position, and character might enable him to appear between God and man, and lay hands upon both. Such we now have in the God-man, Christ Jesus.

(5) HE MAGNIFIED THE LAW AND MADE IT HONORABLE

Man had dishonored it, had cast it off from his neck, and trampled it under his feet. Hence, the first work of Jesus in his mission of restitution was to fulfill all righteousness, whether ceremonial or moral.

"The Lord is well pleased for his righteousness' sake; he will magnify the law, and make it honourable" (Isaiah 42:21).

"Think not that I am come to destroy the law, or the prophets: I am not come to destroy, but to fulfil. For verily I say unto you, Till heaven and earth pass, one jot or one tittle shall in no wise pass from the law, till all be fulfilled. Whosoever therefore shall break one of these least commandments, and shall teach men so, he shall be called the least in the kingdom of heaven: but whosoever shall do and teach them, the same shall be called great in the kingdom of heaven" (Matthew 5:17-19).

The earliest notices of Jesus show his submission to just authority; when he was found in the temple after anxious searching:

"His mother said unto him, Son, why hast thou thus dealt with us? behold, thy father and I have sought thee sorrowing. And he said unto them, How is it that ye sought me? wist ye not that I must be about my Father's business? And they understood not the saying which he spake unto them. And he went down with them, and came to Nazareth, and was subject unto them: but his mother kept all these sayings in her heart. And Jesus increased in wisdom and stature, and in favour with God and man" (Luke 2:48-52).

"Then cometh Jesus from Galilee to Jordan unto John, to be baptized of him. But John forbade him, saying, I have need to be baptized of thee, and comest thou to me? And Jesus answering said unto him, Suffer it to be so now: for thus it becometh us to fulfil all righteousness. Then he suffered him. And Jesus, when he was baptized, went up straightway out of the water: and, lo, the heavens were opened unto him, and he saw the Spirit of God descending like a dove, and lighting upon him: and lo a voice from heaven, saying, This is my beloved Son, in whom I am well pleased" (Matthew 3:13-17).

After his baptism he was "led by the Spirit into the wilderness, being forty days tempted of the devil"; and temptations were multiplied as the days of his public ministry went on. We are told that he "was in all points tempted like as we are, yet without sin" (Hebrews 4:15). The words of the Psalm (40:6, 7, 8) are applied directly to him, and with peculiar fitness:

"Wherefore, when he cometh into the world, he saith, Sacrifice and offering thou wouldest not, but a body hast thou prepared me: in burnt offerings and sacrifices for sin thou hast had no pleasure. Then, said I, Lo, I come (in the volume of the book it is written of me) to do thy will, O God" (Hebrews 10:5-7).

The heathen judge could find no fault in him. Hence it is recorded:

"When Pilate saw that he could prevail nothing, but *that* rather a tumult was made, he took water, and washed *his* hands before the multitude, saying, I am innocent of the blood of this just person: see ye *to it*" (Matthew 27:24).

Thus, from the beginning of life down to the very end, in thought and word and purpose and deed, the will of God was fully and faithfully accepted as the law which he delighted to do, because what God willed was seen and felt to be always and in all things holy and just and infinitely good. Hence, the exhortation of the apostle to believers to imitate his perfect obedience.

"Let this mind be in you, which was also in Christ Jesus: who, being in the form of God, thought it not robbery to be equal with God: but made himself of no reputation, and took upon him the form of a servant, and was made in the likeness of men: and being found in fashion as a man, he humbled himself, and became obedient unto death, even the death of the cross" (Philippians 2:5–8).

He fulfilled both the letter and the spirit of all of the law's requirements. Thus it can be said with the fullest confidence that he "magnified the law and made it honorable"; his holy life and his cheerful obedience set forth in the clearest light the view that he always and in every circumstance had of the excellence of the law, and tended to lead men everywhere, if they will turn their thoughts to his example, to think also of the law of God as worthy of all honor. Those who think of the law, as did Jesus Christ, will have just views of the exceeding folly and sinfulness of sin, and will be most humbly thankful for the wisdom and grace and love that shine forth in the giving of such a Saviour and such a salvation as he has brought to sinful men.

(6) As a Lamb without spot, he offered
himself as a sacrifice for sin

It is now necessary to notice particularly what is called the "High Priesthood of Christ." In order fully to understand this, we need to look back to the office of the high priest under the Mosaic Dispensation on the great Day of Atonement, which was set apart for the holy convocation and for the offering of the appointed sacrifice by the high priest to "make an atonement for the holy sanctuary, and an atonement for the tabernacle of the congregation, and for the altar, and an atonement for the priests, and for all the people of the congregation" (Leviticus 16:33).

Clothed in his holy linen coat and the other holy garments which were put on after washing his flesh with water, he offered first a sin offering for himself and his house. Then he killed the goat of the sin offering for the people, and taking the blood of the offering he entered alone within the vail, into the Holy of Holies, and sprinkled it upon the mercy seat and before the mercy seat (Leviticus 16:15). After this, he confessed all the iniquities and transgressions and sins of the people, putting them on the head of the other goat of the sin offering, which was yet alive, in order that he might "bear upon him all their iniquities into a land not inhabited" (Leviticus 16:20–22). This was to be an everlasting statute unto the people to make an atonement for all their sins once a year.

But the sacrifice which was to be offered by the Great High Priest whom God had appointed was to be offered once for all. As the apostle says:

"For such an high priest became us, *who is* holy, harmless, undefiled, separate from sinners, and made higher than the heavens; who needeth not daily, as those high priests, to offer up sacrifice, first for his own sins, and then for the people's: for this he did once, when he offered up himself. For the law maketh men high priests which have infirmity; but the word of the oath, which was since the law, *maketh* the Son, who is consecrated for evermore" (Hebrews 7:26–28).

Thus Jesus Christ became our substitute. The innocent Lamb of God, as a sacrifice for sin, must come beneath the sword of justice, bearing our sins in his own body on the tree. As God, he was possessed of infinite merit; as sinless man, he could present an acceptable sacrifice. Isaiah brings the scene before us thus:

"Who hath believed our report? and to whom is the arm of the Lord revealed? For he shall grow up before him as a tender plant, and as a root out of a dry ground: he hath no form nor comeliness; and when we shall *see* him, *there is* no beauty that we should desire him. He is despised and rejected of men; a man of sorrows, and acquainted with grief: and we hid as it were *our* faces from him; he was despised, and we esteemed him not. Surely he hath borne our griefs, and carried our sorrows: yet we did esteem him stricken, smitten of God, and afflicted. But he *was* wounded for our transgressions, *he was* bruised for our iniquities: the chastisement of our peace *was* upon him; and with his stripes we are healed. All we like sheep have gone astray; we have turned every one to his own way; and the Lord hath laid on him the iniquity of us all. He was oppressed, and he was afflicted, yet he opened not his mouth: he is brought as a lamb to the slaughter, and as a sheep before her shearers is dumb, so he openeth not his mouth. He was taken from prison and from judgment: and who shall declare his generation? for he was cut off out of the land of the living: for the transgression of *my* people was he stricken. And he made his grave with the wicked, and with the rich in his death; because he had done no violence, neither was any deceit in his mouth. Yet it pleased the Lord to bruise him; he hath put *him* to grief: when thou shalt make his soul an offering for sin, he shall see *his* seed, he shall prolong *his* days, and the pleasure of the Lord shall prosper in his hand. He shall see of the travail of his soul, *and* shall be satisfied: by his knowledge shall my righteous servant justify many; for he shall bear their iniquities. Therefore will I divide him a *portion* with the great and he shall divide the spoil with the strong; because he hath poured out his soul unto death: and he was numbered with the transgressors; and he bare the sin of many, and made intercession for the transgressors" (Isaiah 53:1–12).

Seven hundred years after this prophecy, the Son of God appears upon the cross, in fulfillment of the awful prediction.

> *"With pitying eye the Prince of grace*
> *Beheld our helpless grief;*
> *He saw, and oh, amazing love!*
> *He flew to our relief."*

John, who stood by the cross, tells what he saw in the following language:

"Then Pilate therefore took Jesus, and scourged *him*. And the soldiers platted a crown of thorns, and put *it* on his head, and they put on him a purple robe, and said, Hail, King of the Jews! and they smote him with their hands. Pilate therefore went forth again, and saith unto them, Behold, I bring him forth to you, that ye may know that I find no fault in him. Then came Jesus forth, wearing the crown of thorns, and the purple robe. And *Pilate* saith unto them, Behold the man! When the chief priests therefore and officers saw him, they cried out, saying, Crucify *him*, crucify *him*. Pilate saith unto them, Take ye him, and crucify *him*: for I find no fault in him. The Jews answered him, We have a law, and by our law he ought to die, because he made himself the Son of God.

"When Pilate therefore heard that saying, he was the more afraid; and went again into the judgment hall, and saith unto Jesus, Whence art thou?

But Jesus gave him no answer. Then saith Pilate unto him, Speaketh thou not unto me? knowest thou not that I have power to crucify thee, and have power to release thee? Jesus answered, Thou couldest have no power *at all* against me, except it were given thee from above: therefore he that delivered me unto thee hath the greater sin. And from thenceforth Pilate sought to release him: but the Jews cried out, saying, If thou let this man go, thou art not Cesar's friend: whosoever maketh himself a king speaketh against Cesar.

"When Pilate therefore heard that saying, he brought Jesus forth, and sat down in the judgment seat in a place that is called the Pavement, but in the Hebrew, Gabbatha. And it was the preparation of the passover, and about the sixth hour: and he saith unto the Jews, Behold your King! But they cried out, Away with *him*, away with *him*, crucify him. Pilate saith unto them, Shall I crucify your King? The chief priests answered, We have no king but Cesar. Then delivered he him therefore unto them to be crucified. And they took Jesus, and led *him* away. And he bearing his cross went forth into a place called *the place* of a skull, which is called in the Hebrew Golgotha: where they crucified him, and two others with him, on either side one, and Jesus in the midst.

"And Pilate wrote a title, and put *it* on the cross. And the writing was, JESUS OF NAZARETH THE KING OF THE JEWS. This title then read many of the Jews; for the place where Jesus was crucified was nigh to the city: and it was written in Hebrew, *and* Greek, *and* Latin. Then said the chief priests of the Jews to Pilate, Write not, The King of the Jews; but that he said, I am King of the Jews. Pilate answered, What I have written I have written. Then the soldiers, when they had crucified Jesus, took his garments, and made four parts, to every soldier a part; and also *his* coat: now the coat was without seam, woven from the top throughout. They said therefore among themselves, Let us not rend it, but cast lots for it, whose it shall be: that the Scripture might be fulfilled, which saith, They parted my raiment among them, and for my vesture they did cast lots. These things therefore the soldiers did.

"Now there stood by the cross of Jesus his mother, and his mother's sister, Mary the *wife* of Cleophas, and Mary Magdalene. When Jesus therefore saw his mother, and the disciple standing by, whom he loved, he saith unto his mother, Woman, behold thy son! Then saith he to the disciple, Behold thy mother! And from that hour that disciple took her: unto his own *home*. After this, Jesus knowing that all things were now accomplished, that the Scripture might be fulfilled, saith, I thirst. Now there was set a vessel full of vinegar:

and they filled a sponge with vinegar, and put it upon hyssop, and put it to his mouth. When Jesus therefore had received the vinegar, he said, It is finished: and he bowed his head, and gave up the ghost" (John 19:1–30).

The words of the Lord, "It is finished," are full of meaning.

> "'It is finished!' Oh, what pleasure
>> Do these charming words afford!
> Heavenly blessings, without measure,
>> Flow to us from Christ, the Lord:
>> 'It is finished!'
>> Saints, the dying words record."

Immediately after this cry, the Saviour bowed his head and gave up his spirit. On one occasion, a few months before, he said to some of the Pharisees:

"Therefore doth my Father love me, because I lay down my life, that I might take it again. No man taketh it from me, but I lay it down of myself. I have power to lay it down, and I have power to take it again. This commandment have I received of my Father" (John 10:17, 18).

The giving up of his spirit on the cross was perfectly voluntary on his part, in accordance with what he had previously said. He offered himself as a willing sacrifice, thus completing his earthly work.

(7) THE RESURRECTION OF CHRIST

It is interesting to notice what stress is laid in the New Testament on the resurrection of Christ. The sacred writers were deeply impressed with the importance of testifying to those to whom they preached the gospel, that, after his death on the cross and his burial in the new tomb of Joseph of Arimathea, Jesus rose from the dead, and to present to them clear proofs of the wonderful fact.

They were able to do this, because special pains were taken by the Jews to guard against the removal of his body by his disciples, and the spreading abroad of a false report of his return to life.

"Now the next day, that followed the day of the preparation, the chief priests and Pharisees came together unto Pilate, saying, Sir, we remember that that deceiver said, while he was yet alive, After three days I will rise again. Command therefore that the sepulchre be made sure until the third day, lest his disciples come by night, and steal him away, and say unto the people, He is risen from the dead: so the last error shall be worse than the first. Pilate said unto them, Ye have a watch: go your way, make it as sure as ye can. So they went, and made the sepulchre sure, sealing the stone and setting a watch" (Matthew 27:62–66).

It was true that Jesus again and again had foretold his rising from the dead. The first instance was early in his ministry as appears from his reply to the Jews:

"Then answered the Jews and said unto him, What sign shewest thou unto us, seeing that thou doest these things? Jesus answered and said unto them, Destroy this temple, and in three days I will raise it up. Then said the Jews, Forty and six years was this temple in building, and wilt thou rear it up in three days? But he spake of the temple of his body. When therefore he was risen from the dead, his disciples remembered that he had said this unto them; and they believed the Scripture, and the word which Jesus had said" (John 2:18–22).

The Evangelist John testifies to the prophecy of Jesus and to the effect produced on the minds of the disciples when, after seeing and conversing with him and handling him, they saw that his words were strictly true. The last occasion on which he made the prophecy of his resurrection was just before the fearful agony in the garden and his seizure by the Jews.

"And when they had sung a hymn, they went out into the mount of Olives. Then saith Jesus unto them, All ye shall be offended because of me this night: for it is written, I will smite the Shepherd, and the sheep of the flock shall be scattered abroad. But after I am risen again, I will go before you into Galilee" (Matthew 26:30–32).

The Apostle Paul uses very strong language when writing of the gospel which he had preached to the Corinthians, of the facts that he had made known to them, and of the importance especially of the resurrection of Christ.

"Moreover, brethren, I declare unto you the gospel which I preached unto you, which also ye have received, and wherein ye stand; by which also ye are saved, if ye keep in memory what I preached unto you, unless ye have believed in vain. For I delivered unto you first of all that which I also received, how that Christ died for our sins according to the Scriptures; and that he was buried, and that he rose again the third day according to the Scriptures; and that he was seen of Cephas, then of the twelve: after that, he was seen of above five hundred brethren at once; of whom the greater part remain unto this present, but some are fallen asleep. After that, he was seen of James; then of all the apostles. And last of all he was seen of me also, as of one born out of due time. For I am the least of the apostles, that am not meet to be called an apostle, because I persecuted the church of God. But by the grace of God I am what I am: and his grace which *was bestowed* upon me was not in vain; but I laboured more abundantly than they all; yet not I, but the grace of God which was with me. Therefore whether *it were* I or they, so we preach, and so ye believed. Now if Christ be preached that he rose from the dead, how say some among you that there is no resurrection of the dead? But if there be no resurrection of the dead, then is Christ not risen: and if Christ be not risen, then is our preaching vain, and your faith is also vain. Yea, and we are found false witnesses of God; because we have testified of God that he raised up Christ: whom he raised not up, if so be that the dead rise not. For if the dead rise not, then is not Christ raised: and if Christ be not raised, your faith is vain; ye are yet in your sins. Then they also that are fallen asleep in Christ are perished. If only in this life we have hope in Christ, we are of all men most miserable. But now is Christ risen from the dead, and become the first fruits of them that slept" (1 Corinthians 15:1–20).

It will be seen that from the resurrection of Christ there followed several exceedingly important results.

It established his perfect truthfulness. He had foretold that he would rise again within a specified time, and also within a very brief time. As he went out to the Mount of Olives, he had made a distinct promise to his disciples that, after rising again, he would go before them into Galilee. Some of them seem to have been very slow of understanding. For as Peter, James, and John came down with the Lord from the mount of transfiguration—

"He charged them that they should tell no man what things they had seen, till the Son of man were risen from the dead. And they kept that saying with themselves, questioning one with another what the rising from the dead should mean" (Mark 9:9, 10).

But after the promise made on the way to the Mount of Olives, they probably had more correct views. All that he had said to them would probably be remembered, and the fulfillment of his promise was a convincing proof of his truthfulness. They would naturally say of every other gracious word that he had spoken: "This is a faithful saying, and worthy of all acceptation." A failure to fulfill one promise would have opened the way in their minds to doubts as to all his promises and all of his teaching.

Again, Jesus Christ was "declared to be the Son of God, with power, according to the Spirit of holiness, by the resurrection from the dead." It was God's testimony to his Sonship, and to his own full satisfaction with what Jesus had done as the substitute of sinners in bearing their sin in his own body on the cross.

The way thus was prepared for calling on men to believe on the Lord Jesus, with a faith firm, strong, and that cannot be shaken—a faith that honors God our Saviour and gives rest to the troubled soul.

(8) The work of the Great High Priest in heaven

After the Lord's resurrection a number of interesting facts are recorded,

"Of all that Jesus began both to do and teach, until the day in which he was taken up, after that he through the Holy Ghost had given commandments unto the apostles whom he had chosen: to whom also he shewed himself alive after his passion by many infallible proofs, being seen of them forty days, and speaking of the things pertaining to the kingdom of God" (Acts 1:1-3).

His last meeting with his disciples illustrates his deep concern for them, and for the work which he entrusted to their hands, now that he was just on the eve of his departure from them to take up and carry on his high-priestly and royal work in heaven. While they were gathered in Jerusalem he suddenly appeared in their midst. They were terrified and affrighted, supposing that they had seen a spirit. But he showed them his feet and his hands, and did eat before them, in order to prove that he was not a spirit, but their risen Lord.

"Then opened he their understanding, that they might understand the Scriptures. And said unto them, Thus it is written, and thus it behooved Christ to suffer, and to rise from the dead the third day: and that repentance and remission of sins should be preached in his name among all nations, beginning at Jerusalem. And ye are witnesses of these things. And, behold, I send the promise of my Father upon you: but tarry ye in the city of Jerusalem, until ye be endued with power from on high.

"And he led them out as far as to Bethany, and he lifted up his hands, and blessed them. And it came to pass, while he blessed them, he was parted from them, and carried up into heaven. And they worshipped him, and returned to Jerusalem with great joy: and were continually in the temple, praising and blessing God" (Luke 24:45-53).

As one has well said: "'While he blessed them, he was parted from them and carried up into heaven,' and ever since he has continued to shower blessings upon them." It is well for the believer to give diligent heed to the exhortation:

"Let us run with patience the race that is set before us, looking unto Jesus the author and finisher of our faith, who for the joy that was set before him endured the cross, despising the shame, and is set down at the right hand of the throne of God" (Hebrews 12:1, 2).

This exhortation directs the attention of believers to Jesus, the "Captain" of our faith, as it is translated in the margin of the Revised Version, as one who led the way in the same path of faith that his people are called to tread; it directs their eye to him as having reached the end to which his faith looked, and presents him also as the "Finisher," or Perfecter, of their faith, leading them on until they rejoice, receiving the end of their faith, even the salvation of their souls (1 Peter 1:9). It directs their eyes to him, not only on the cross, but also to him in heaven at the right hand of the throne of God as their High Priest, performing there his gracious and effectual work on their behalf. Let us therefore look to this High Priest.

"Wherefore, holy brethren, partakers of the heavenly calling, consider the Apostle and High Priest of our profession, Christ Jesus: who was faithful to him that appointed him, as also Moses was *faithful* in all his house" (Hebrews 3:1, 2).

"For every high priest taken from among men is ordained for men in things *pertaining* to God, that he may offer both gifts and sacrifices for sins.

"And no man taketh this honour unto himself, but he that is called of God, as *was* Aaron. So also Christ glorified not himself to be made a high priest; but he that said unto him, Thou art my Son, to day have I begotten thee. As he saith also in another *place*, Thou *art* a priest for ever after the order of Melchisedec. Who in the days of his flesh, when he had offered up prayers and supplications with strong crying and tears unto him that was able to save him from death, and was heard in that he feared; though he were a Son, yet learned he obedience by the things which he suffered: and being made perfect, he became the author of eternal salvation unto all them that obey him; called of God a high priest after the order of Melchisedec" (Hebrews 5:1, 4–10).

"For men verily swear by the greater: and an oath for confirmation *is* to them an end of all strife. Wherein God, willing more abundantly to shew unto the heirs of promise the immutability of his counsel, confirmed *it* by an oath: that by two immutable things, in which *it was* impossible for God to lie, we might have a strong consolation, who have fled for refuge to lay hold upon the hope set before us: which *hope* we have as an anchor of the soul, both sure and stedfast, and which entereth into that within the vail; whither the forerunner is for us entered, *even* Jesus, made a high priest for ever after the order of Melchisedec" (Hebrews 6:16–20).

"But this *man*, because he continueth ever, hath an unchangeable priest-hood. Wherefore he is able also to save them to the uttermost that come unto God by him, seeing he ever liveth to make intercession for them. For such a high priest became us, *who is* holy, harmless, undefiled, separate from sinners, and made higher than the heavens; who needeth not daily, as those high priests, to offer up sacrifice, first for his own sins, and then for the people's: for this he did once, when he offered up himself. For the law maketh men high priests which have infirmity; but the word of the oath, which was since the law, *maketh* the Son, who is consecrated [or, *'perfected,'* as in the Revised Version] for evermore" (Hebrews 7:24–28).

"Now of the things which we have spoken *this* is the sum: We have such a high priest, who is set on the right hand of the throne of the Majesty in the heavens: a minister of the sanctuary, and of the true tabernacle, which the Lord pitched, and not man. For every high priest is ordained to offer gifts and sacrifices: wherefore *it is* of necessity that this man have somewhat also to offer" (Hebrews 8:1–3).

"But Christ being come a high priest of good things to come, by a greater and more perfect tabernacle, not made with hands, that is to say, not of this building; neither by the blood of goats and calves, but by his own blood he entered in once into the holy place, having obtained eternal redemption *for* us. For if the blood of bulls and of goats, and the ashes of a heifer sprinkling the unclean, sanctifieth to the purifying of the flesh; how much more shall the blood of Christ, who through the eternal Spirit offered himself without spot to God, purge your conscience from dead works to serve the living God?" (Hebrews 9:11–14).

"For Christ is not entered into the holy places made with hands, *which are* the figures of the true; but into heaven itself, now to appear in the presence of God for us: nor yet that he should offer himself often, as the high priest entereth into the holy place every year with blood of others; for then must he often have suffered since the foundation of the world: but now once in the end of the world hath he appeared to put away sin by the *sacrifice* of himself. And as it is appointed unto men once to die, but after this the judgment: so Christ *was* once offered to bear the sins of many; and unto them that look for him shall he appear the second time without sin unto salvation" (Hebrews 9:24–28).

From these passages we learn (1) that Christ did not take the office of high priest upon himself, but was appointed by God; (2) that he was a priest "after the order of Melchisedec, and not after the order of Aaron"; (3) that he had an unchangeable high priesthood—that is, the office did not pass from one to another as the years rolled on, but he was a high priest forever; (4) that he ever liveth to make intercession for those on whose behalf he ministers; it is "Jesus Christ the same yesterday, and to-day, and forever" (Hebrews 13:8); (5) that Christ is entered "into heaven itself, now to appear in the presence of God for us"; (6) that he entered there, not "by the blood of goats and calves, but by his own blood"; (7) that by this one entry by his own blood he has "obtained eternal redemption for us"; (8) that "by two immutable things, in which it was impossible for God to lie," we have "strong consolation," having "fled for refuge to lay hold upon the hope set before us: which hope we have as an anchor of the soul, both sure and steadfast, and which entereth into that within the vail; whither the forerunner is for us entered, even Jesus"; (9) that "unto them that look for him shall he appear the second time without sin unto salvation." Dr. A. C. Kendrick[1] says: "'Without (apart from) sin'—not without the contamination of sin, for that he never had; not without temptation to sin, though this will be true; but here, in apparent contrast to 'bearing the sins of many,' he will come without the burden of sin upon him: that burden which made him a man of sorrows, which compelled him to endure temptation in the wilderness, agonize in the garden, and shed his blood on the cross."

The gospel sets before us such a High Priest; who has made such an offering for sin; who has entered heaven on our behalf; who ever lives to make intercession for us; through whom we have strong consolation, and a hope like an anchor firmly fixed within the vail where Jesus is. What a plan of

---

1. "Commentary on the Epistle to the Hebrews," American Baptist Publication Society, Philadelphia.

salvation, and what a Saviour we have here presented! What thanks should be rendered to God for his unspeakable gift?

There is also another portion of the Lord's work in heaven, which is not so often referred to as his work as High Priest—his work as King. In order to gain a clear understanding of this, we must refer to what is said of the position he holds in heaven, and of the authority entrusted to his hands, and of the parties for whose benefit he wields that authority.

"God, who at sundry times and in divers manners spake in time past unto the fathers by the prophets, hath in these last days spoken unto us by *his* Son, whom he hath appointed heir of all things, by whom also he made the worlds; who being the brightness of *his* glory, and the express image of his person, and upholding all things by the word of his power, when he had by himself purged our sins, sat down on the right hand of the Majesty on high; being made so much better than the angels, as he hath by inheritance obtained *a* more excellent name than they. For unto which of the angels said he at any time, Thou art my Son, this day have I begotten thee? And again, I will be to him a Father, and he shall be to me a Son? And again, when he bringeth in the firstbegotten into the world, he saith, And let all the angels of God worship him. And of the angels he saith, Who maketh his angels spirits, and his ministers a flame of fire.

"But unto the Son *he saith,* Thy throne, O God, is for ever and ever: a sceptre of righteousness *is* the sceptre of thy kingdom. Thou hast loved righteousness, and hated iniquity; therefore God, *even* thy God, hath anointed thee with the oil of gladness above thy fellows. And, Thou, Lord, in the beginning hast laid the foundation of the earth; and the heavens are the works of thine hands. They shall perish, but thou remainest: and they all shall wax old as doth a garment; and as a vesture shalt thou fold them up, and they shall be changed: but thou art the same, and thy years shall not fail.

"But to which of the angels said he at any time, Sit on my right hand, until I make thine enemies thy footstool? Are they not all ministering spirits, sent forth to minister for them who shall be heirs of salvation?" (Hebrews 1:1–14).

"Wherefore I also, after I heard of your faith in the Lord Jesus, and love unto all the saints, cease not to give thanks for you, making mention of you in my prayers; that the God of our Lord Jesus Christ, the Father of glory, may give unto you the spirit of wisdom and revelation in the knowledge of him: the eyes of your understanding being enlightened; that ye may know

what is the hope of his calling, and what the riches of the glory of his inheritance in the saints, and what is the exceeding greatness of his power to
us-ward who believe, according to the working of his mighty power, which
he wrought in Christ, when he raised him from the dead, and set him at his
own right hand in the heavenly *places*, far above all principality, and power,
and might, and dominion, and every name that is named, not only in this
world, but also in that which is to come: and hath put all *things* under his feet,
and gave him *to be* the head over *all things* to the church, which is his body,
the fulness of him that filleth all in all" (Ephesians 1:15-23).

These statements are in full harmony with the words of the Lord himself when he gave the Great Commission to his disciples on the mountain
in Galilee.

"All power [or, as in the Revised Version, '*all authority*'] is given unto me
in heaven and in earth" (Matthew 28:18).

Such is the exaltation of the Lord Jesus Christ. In view of this, what point
and impressiveness is given to the question of our Lord to his disciples on
their way to Emmaus:

"O fools, and slow of heart to believe all that the prophets have spoken:
ought not Christ to have suffered these things, and to enter into his glory?"
(Luke 24:25, 26).

The meaning of these statements would seem to be perfectly clear to
any ordinary mind. There are certain things to be noticed in regard to "the
church," the Lord's "body." The word church includes all who are, in the
strong language of the Scriptures, "in Christ"; all who have by faith in him
become united with him. In looking back on the past we see a long line of
these members of "the church," the Lord's "body," scattered hither and thither
"in the world." In looking forward to the future, we see the same long line
extending down to the end of the world, the members of Christ's church still
scattered among the nations. The Lord, on the eve of his crucifixion, looking
at those of his own about him and at those then dwelling on the earth, and
at those who were yet to believe on him through their words, was deeply
concerned for them. He knew the hatred of the world for his people, and saw
all the various forms of evil that they must meet in their course through life.
But he did not propose to take them with him at once out of the world. He
uttered a memorable prayer for them:

"I pray not that thou shouldest take them out of the world, but that thou shouldest keep them from the evil. They are not of the world, even as I am not of the world. ... Neither pray I for these alone, but for them also which shall believe on me through their word" (John 17:15, 16; 20).

There was a work for them to do, a work to be done amidst suffering and toil and danger. He knew it all from his own personal experience. He knew also what they needed to nerve them for the work and suffering and various trials before them. Hence, when he met his own on the mountain in Galilee, he first pointed them to the lofty position to which he was about to be raised:

"All power is given unto me in heaven and in earth" (Matthew 28:18).

Then the command that they were to obey was given. It was with special relation to his church and to the daily and hourly necessities and emergencies of its members, that all things were put beneath the feet of Jesus Christ, their elder brother, and that he was given to be Head over all things. Dr. J. A. Smith[2] says: "The purpose of the exaltation is here made known. It is in the interest of human redemption that all this is done. In this it is provided that there shall be no possibility of opposition or hostility in any quarter with ability to mar in any way the perfection of the plan, or hinder or delay its execution." Under the supreme authority of him who is "the way and the truth and the life," every purpose embraced in the plan of redemption that Infinite Wisdom devised shall be carried on to its fullest completion; and every interest of his church, even of the weakest of its members, shall be carefully guarded, and every event of their lives made to work together for their good. How wise and how gracious the plan of God's redemption, and how complete the array of means for carrying it on until that promised day, when out of heaven a great voice shall be heard saying:

"Behold, the tabernacle of God is with men, and he will dwell with them, and they shall be his people, and God himself shall be with them, *and be* their God. And God shall wipe away all tears from their eyes; and there shall be no more death, neither sorrow, nor crying, neither shall there be any more pain: for the former things are passed away" (Revelation 21:3, 4).

---

2. "Commentary on the Epistle to the Ephesians" (1:22), American Baptist Publication Society, Philadelphia.

5

Gifts Flowing from the Grace of God

In order that we may understand the aboundings of the grace of God, there are several subjects that need to be carefully examined; these may be fitly grouped together in this chapter.

(1) ELECTION

This subject will lead us back far beyond the coming of the beloved Son of God into the world; beyond the deliverance of the children of Israel from the bondage in Egypt; beyond the early date when the gracious promises of God were made to Abraham, the father of the faithful; beyond the wonderful events that are described in the opening chapters of the book of Genesis; beyond that "beginning" in which God created the heavens and the earth. We shall find it necessary to turn to statements made in the volume of divine truth concerning the earliest recorded purposes of God. Among these we find mention of a doctrine that has awakened a great deal of hostile feeling in unrenewed hearts.

By election we understand God's choice of individuals of the sinful race of man to become possessors of eternal life through Jesus Christ our Lord. It is a wonderful thought that, before the foundation of the world, God made such a purpose, and that through all the ages of this world that purpose has been steadily carried out. Let us proceed to notice what God has taught us on this subject in his holy word:

"Blessed *be* the God and Father of our Lord Jesus Christ, who hath blessed us with all spiritual blessings in heavenly *places* in Christ: according as he hath chosen us in him before the foundation of the world, that we should be holy and without blame before him in love: having predestinated us unto the adoption of children by Jesus Christ to himself, according to the good pleasure of his will. To the praise of the glory of his grace, wherein he hath made us accepted in the beloved: in whom we have redemption through his blood, the forgiveness of sins, according to the riches of his grace; wherein he hath abounded toward us in all wisdom and prudence; having made known unto us the mystery of his will, according to his good pleasure which he hath purposed in himself: that in the dispensation of the fulness of times he might gather together in one all things in Christ, both which are in heaven, and which are on earth; *even* in him: in whom also we have obtained an inheritance, being predestinated according to the purpose of him who worketh all things after the counsel of his own will: that we should be to the praise of his glory, who first trusted in Christ. In whom ye also *trusted,* after that ye heard the word of truth, the gospel of your salvation: in whom also, after that ye believed, ye were sealed with that Holy Spirit of promise, which is the earnest of our inheritance until the redemption of the purchased possession, unto the praise of his glory" (Ephesians 1:3–12).

"And we know that all things work together for good to them that love God, to them who are the called according to *his* purpose. For whom he did foreknow, he also did predestinate *to be* conformed to the image of his Son, that he might be the firstborn among many brethren. Moreover, whom he did predestinate, them he also called: and whom he called, them he also justified: and whom he justified, them he also glorified. What shall we then say to these things? If God *be* for us, who *can be* against us? He that spared not his own Son, but delivered him up for us all, how shall he not with him also freely *give* us all things? Who shall lay any thing to the charge of God's elect? *It is* God that justifieth. Who *is* he that condemneth? *It is* Christ that died, yea rather, that is risen again, who is even at the right hand of God, who also maketh intercession for us. Who shall separate us from the love of Christ? *shall* tribulation, or distress, or persecution, or famine, or nakedness, or peril, or sword? As it is written, For thy sake we are killed all the day long; we are accounted as sheep for the slaughter. Nay, in all these things we are more than conquerors through him that loved us. For I am persuaded, that neither death, nor life, nor angels, nor principalities, nor powers, nor things present, nor things to come, nor height, nor depth, nor any other creature, shall be able to separate us from the love of God, which is in Christ Jesus our Lord" (Romans 8:28–39).

The Lord himself has taught us what shall transpire on that happy day when the gracious purpose of God, formed so long before, shall be fully accomplished.

"When the Son of man shall come in his glory, and all the holy angels with him, then shall he sit upon the throne of his glory: and before him shall be gathered all nations: and he shall separate them one from another, as a shepherd divideth *his* sheep from the goats: and he shall set the sheep on his right hand, but the goats on the left. Then shall the King *say* unto them on his right hand, Come, ye blessed of my Father, inherit the kingdom prepared for you from the foundation of the world" (Matthew 25:31–34).

These few passages present a fair view of the truth on this important subject. We see the purpose of God dating far back before the foundation of this world, before there had yet risen on it the sun and the moon by whose aid our days and months and years are measured. They tell us of God's purpose, choice, election, and predestination long before the creation of any one of those who were thus to be brought to the kingdom prepared for them from the foundation of the world. If we ask why they were chosen and others were left, we find that no answer to the question has been given by him who alone can explain his reasons. It becomes us, then, to rest content with what it has seemed good to him to reveal. We, with all the light that has been thrown on the character of God in these days, when the true light shineth, ought certainly to feel as did Abraham when he said: "Shall not the Judge of all the earth do right?" Let us therefore bow reverently before him, saying: "Even so, Father, for so it seemed good in thy sight." Of this one thing we may be perfectly sure, that God's election gives no encouragement whatever for any one to continue in sin. The elect, God did "predestinate to be conformed to the image of his Son," to the image of him who is the brightness of the Father's glory and the express image of his person. These words, as also the following words of Paul, are decisive on this point:

"But we are bound to give thanks always to God for you, brethren beloved of the Lord, because God hath from the beginning chosen you to salvation through sanctification of the Spirit and belief of the truth: whereunto he called you by our gospel, to the obtaining of the glory of our Lord Jesus Christ" (2 Thessalonians 2:13, 14).

Salvation, as that word is used in the Scriptures, is always salvation from sin; the predestination of God always means his sovereign purpose that they shall be conformed to the image of his Son.

(2) REGENERATION

When the Lord was conversing with Nicodemus, he made to him a statement that startled him, as it has startled many men since.

"Jesus answered and said unto him, Verily, verily, I say unto thee, Except a man be born again, he cannot see the kingdom of God. Nicodemus saith unto him, How can a man be born when he is old? can he enter the second time into his mother's womb, and be born? Jesus answered, Verily, verily, I say unto thee, Except a man be born of water and *of* the Spirit, he cannot enter into the kingdom of God. That which is born of the flesh is flesh; and that which is born of the Spirit is spirit. Marvel not that I said unto thee, Ye must be born again. The wind bloweth where it listeth, and thou hearest the sound thereof, but canst not tell whence it cometh, and whither it goeth: so is every one that is born of the Spirit" (John 3:38).

From this brief passage we learn what is also distinctly taught elsewhere in different form—that the sinner cannot by any means work out a salvation for himself. In the emphatic words of the apostle to the Ephesians, he says:

"And you hath he quickened [that is, *made alive*] who were dead in trespasses and sins. But God who is rich in mercy, for his great love wherewith he loved us, hath quickened us [that is, *made us alive*] together with Christ (by grace ye are saved;) and hath raised us up together, and made us to sit together in heavenly places in Christ Jesus: that in the ages to come he might show the exceeding riches of his grace, in his kindness toward us, through Christ Jesus" (Ephesians 2:1, 4–7).

The sinner can no more make himself alive from his death in trespasses and sins than could Lazarus raise himself to life when lying in his tomb, his body hastening to decay. Many a sinner who has thought he could work out a salvation for himself has found all his hope of helping himself vanish when confronted with the words of the Lord: "Ye must be born again."

We learn from these passages of Scripture that it is God, and God only, who quickens those who are spiritually dead, and makes them alive together with Christ. But Jesus does not answer all the questions that may be asked as to how this is done. His language to Nicodemus seems to be meant as a rebuke to him and to all others who may ask how spiritual life is given. He likens the process to the blowing of the wind, in regard to which they cannot tell whence it cometh, or whither it goeth, and says: "So is every one that is born of the Spirit." We should have thought it strange if Mary and Martha, or the centurion of Capernaum, or the widow of Nain, had troubled Jesus with questions as to how he had brought their dead back to life again. It was enough to know that their loved ones lived once more, but it was by no means necessary to know how he had raised them to life again. They knew them to be alive, and that was enough. So those who are raised from spiritual death and made partakers of spiritual life, should not spend any moments of that new life in asking useless questions, but rather busy themselves with devout thanks for the gift, and in earnest efforts to make the most of their life for the glory of the gracious Giver. It will be well to notice and bear in mind that this new birth is the first step toward the fulfillment of God's gracious purpose in regard to those whom he had chosen before the foundation of the world.

(3) Repentance

By this is meant a true godly sorrow for sin; that is, a sorrow which arises from the understanding that sin, in its worst forms, is an act of disobedience or of positive enmity to God, who demands our best obedience, and who is worthy to be loved by all men with all their heart and soul and might and mind and strength. But Paul says:

"The carnal mind is enmity against God; for it is not subject to the law of God, neither indeed can be" (Romans 8:7).

David, after his fearful crimes against Uriah and his wife, was brought to real godly sorrow, for he said:

"Have mercy upon me, O God, according to thy lovingkindness: according unto the multitude of thy tender mercies blot out my transgressions. Wash me thoroughly from mine iniquity, and cleanse me from my sin. For I acknowledge my transgressions: and my sin is ever before me. Against thee, thee only, have I sinned, and done this evil in thy sight" (Psalm 51:14).

He did not mean to say that he had committed no crime against his faithful soldier and his wife; but his sense of the majesty and glory of God, and of the obedience that was due to him, was so great that, for the time being, he was overwhelmed with shame and sorrow on that account, and appears scarcely able to think of anything else.

It will be seen that there is in a sinner's repentance toward God a new view, and a true view, of the character of God and what is due to him, and also a new view, and a true view, of himself and of the folly and wickedness of his own wrong thoughts of God, of his neglect of him, his disobedience and his enmity to him. This is a complete change of mind in regard to God, and in regard to what his own feelings and conduct toward God ought to have been. A great change has taken place when one can say: "What God says of himself and of his just claims, and of me and of my opposition to these claims, is all true." One who can say this cannot help feeling deep sorrow and a real desire to make a change, which means a real desire to lead a new life, in which God's will shall rule and his will shall be submitted to the will of God. All this means confession, honest confession of sin, which is simply saying about his former life, his thoughts and feelings and actions toward God, exactly what God says about them. This is what is meant by John when he writes:

"If we confess our sins, he is faithful and just to forgive us our sins, and to cleanse us from all unrighteousness" (1 John 1:9).

(4) Faith—faith in God, faith in the Lord Jesus Christ

It was a want of faith in God that led to the first departure of man from him, and to the long and fearful separation between the Fount of Blessing and those who always need the blessings which can only come from that Fount. In order that there may be a return to God, men need to have their faith in him restored. The Apostle Paul says:

"Whosoever shall call upon the name of the Lord shall be saved. How then shall they call on him in whom they have not believed? and how shall they believe in him of whom they have not heard? and how shall they hear without a preacher?" (Romans 10:13, 14).

This teaches us that to be saved there must be a preaching, a hearing, a believing, and a calling on the name of God; that is, the truth about God must be proclaimed, be heard, and be believed. As we have seen, the truth about God, preached, heard, and believed, led to repentance.

So, in regard to faith in the Lord Jesus Christ, there must be the same process, the proclaiming of the truth about him and his work that has been taught in the Bible, the hearing of that truth, the believing of it, in order to the calling on the Lord. God does not ask sinners, when they feel their need of cleansing and salvation, to bow themselves to the ground and call on some being of whom they have never heard. But he has prepared the anxious sinner's way by bearing clear and full testimony to his own love in sending his Son, to the character of his well-beloved Son, to the work that his Son undertook and finished, to his willingness and his ability to save to the uttermost whosoever calleth on the name of the Lord. What, then, is meant by faith in the Lord Jesus Christ? It is a belief of all that God has taught and caused to be proclaimed to men concerning the Saviour and the salvation that his love has provided; and an earnest, honest calling on the Lord. That earnest and honest calling on the Lord means that all dependence on any thing else than what Christ Jesus has done is utterly renounced, and that in Christ is all his desire, all his trust, all his hope. In confession of his sin, the sinner sets to his seal that what God has said of his guilt and his lost condition is true. In his exercise of faith in Jesus Christ, he in like manner sets to his seal that all which God has promised—a full and final salvation from the guilt, the defilement, and the power of sin—is fully, unalterably true. How truly it may be said that one exercising such a faith no longer walks in darkness, but that to him the words of John may be justly applied:

"But if we walk in the light, as he is in the light, we have fellowship one with another, and the blood of Jesus Christ his Son cleanseth us from all sin" (1 John 1:7).

(5) JUSTIFICATION

This subject deals with the momentous question, "How shall a man be just with God?" Those who are not "just with God" can have no share in the mansions that Christ is to prepare for his followers in heaven, or part in the glory that will crown them there. Hence the importance of a correct answer to the question. We must seek such an answer in the pages of the Sacred Scriptures. It is from these alone that we learn that it is possible for a sinner ever to stand justified before God, the Infinitely Holy One; and the only reliable statement as to how a sinner can be just with God must come from God himself. Let us gather together some of those passages which give us the mind of God on this subject.

In the first place, we are told that there are things "from which ye could not be justified by the law of Moses" (Acts 13:39); also things that "the law could not do, in that it was weak through the flesh" (Romans 8:3). It is in vain, therefore, to look for justification by the law of Moses. The law can, and does, condemn the transgressor; and that is all that it can do. There are some who may vainly imagine that they can present some good works that may have some part in their justification. But let us see what the word of God says to such:

"For whosoever shall keep the whole law, and yet offend in one *point*, he is guilty of all" (James 2:10).

"Where is boasting then? It is excluded. By what law? of works? Nay; but by the law of faith. Therefore we conclude that a man is justified by faith without the deeds of the law" (Romans 3:27, 28).

"And if by grace, then is it no more of works: otherwise grace is no more grace. But if it be of works, then is it no more grace: otherwise work is no more work" (Romans 11:6).

From these passages we learn that it is impossible for a sinner, even if he has transgressed the law only once, to bring any of his supposed good works before God, and hope to secure justification because of them. Even under earthly governments, one murder or one theft makes him a transgressor; and his transgression calls for his condemnation, and no number of good deeds will induce the jury and the court to justify him. This is especially true under the government of God; for even one sin shows that the sinner's heart is not right in the sight of God. If, then, all of the sinner's works are shut out, we must ask what way of justification the word of God makes known to us.

"Be it known unto you therefore, men and brethren, that through this man is preached unto you the forgiveness of sins: and by him all that believe are justified from all things, from which ye could not be justified by the law of Moses" (Acts 13:38, 39).

"There is therefore now no condemnation to them which are in Christ Jesus, who walk not after the flesh, but after the Spirit. For the law of the Spirit of life in Jesus Christ hath made me free from the law of sin and death. For what the law could not do, in that it was weak through the flesh, God sending his own Son in the likeness of sinful flesh, and for sin, condemned sin in the flesh: that the righteousness of the law might be fulfilled in us, who walk not after the flesh, but after the Spirit" (Romans 8:1-4).

"Verily, verily, I say unto you, He that heareth my word, and believeth on him that sent me, hath everlasting life, and shall not come into condemnation; but is passed from death unto life" (John 5:24).

"Now we know that what things soever the law saith, it saith to them who are under the law: that every mouth may be stopped, and all the world may become guilty before God. Therefore by the deeds of the law there shall no flesh be justified in his sight: for by the law is the knowledge of sin. But now the righteousness of God without the law is manifested, being witnessed by the law and the prophets; even the righteousness of God *which is* by faith of Jesus Christ unto all and upon all them that believe; for there is no difference: for all have sinned, and come short of the glory of God, being justified freely by his grace through the redemption that is in Christ Jesus: whom God hath set forth *to be* a propitiation through faith in his blood, to declare his righteousness for the remission of sins that are past, through the forbearance of God; to declare, *I say*, at this time his righteousness: that he might be just, and the justifier of him which believeth in Jesus. Where is boasting then? It is excluded. By what law? of works? Nay; but by the law of faith. Therefore we conclude that a man is justified by faith without the deeds of the law" (Romans 3:19–28).

"Therefore being justified by faith, we have peace with God through our Lord Jesus Christ: by whom also we have access by faith into this grace wherein we stand, and rejoice in hope of the glory of God" (Romans 5:1, 2).

It would seem that special care had been taken in order that no one might mistake the richness and fullness of the grace of God in providing for the justification of those that trust in Jesus Christ. Hence we copy more largely the words of surprising grace:

"For if by one man's offence death reigned by one; much more they which received abundance of grace and of the gift of righteousness shall reign in life by one, Jesus Christ. Therefore, as by the offence of one *judgment came* upon all men to condemnation; even so by the righteousness of one *the free gift came* upon all men unto justification of life. For as by one man's disobedience many were made sinners, so by the obedience of one shall many be made righteous. Moreover the law entered, that the offence might abound. But where sin abounded, grace did much more abound: that as sin hath reigned unto death, even so might grace reign through righteousness unto eternal life by Jesus Christ our Lord" (Romans 5:17–21).

It must be further noticed that this grace, this glorious gift, comes to men through Jesus Christ, and through no other channel:

"But of him are ye in Christ Jesus, who of God is made unto us wisdom, and righteousness, and sanctification, and redemption" (1 Corinthians 1:30).

"Now then we are ambassadors for Christ, as though God did beseech *you* by us: we pray you in Christ's stead, be ye reconciled to God. For he hath made him *to be* sin for us, who knew no sin; that we might be made the righteousness of God in him" (2 Corinthians 5:20, 21).

In these passages, and in others that are found in the Scriptures, it appears that justification is the act of God. This is stated distinctly in Romans 8:33, whether we take the translation of the Common Version as correct, "It is God that justifieth," or whether we accept that of the margin of the Revised Version as preferable, "Shall God that justifieth?" Both of them admit that to justify belongs to God, and that when he justifies there is no possibility of condemnation from any other source. The ground of justification is found in the work, the whole of the work, of the Son of God, whom God "gave that whosoever believeth in him should not perish, but have everlasting life." What a ground the Father hath given us for the fullest belief in Christ! What reason for devout thankfulness the redeemed have! What a motive to induce them to live, not unto themselves, but unto him who has brought to them a salvation so helpful and so glorious!

(6) Sanctification

The subjects that we have been considering in this chapter are all directly connected with the salvation for sinners by the grace of God. That salvation, in order to be complete, must include everything that is necessary to deliver the sinner from the condemnation and punishment that properly follow sin; from that defilement of the heart and conscience which sin causes; and thus to restore the sinner to the image and favor of God, the Infinitely Holy One. Unless all this is brought about, there can be no salvation. A mere forgiveness of all past sins, with no regeneration, repentance, faith in God and in his beloved Son, putting off the old man and putting on the new man, would be no real salvation, and could bring no real enduring blessing. If any sinner should be ready to satisfy himself with such a salvation, any one who had really heard Christ, and been taught by him, would be very ready to inform him as to what is demanded by the Scriptures:

"As the truth is in Jesus, that ye put off concerning the former conversation the old man, which is corrupt according to the deceitful lusts; and be renewed in the spirit of your mind; and that ye put on the new man, which after God is created in righteousness and true holiness" (Ephesians 4:21-24).

The prayer of Jesus just before he went out to the Garden of Gethsemane, shows his tender solicitude for those disciples who were with him, and for all others down to the end of the world.

"They are not of the world, even as I am not of the world. Sanctify them through thy truth: thy word is truth. As thou hast sent me into the world, even so have I also sent them into the world. And for their sakes I sanctify myself, that they also might be sanctified through the truth. Neither pray I for these alone, but for them also which shall believe on me through their word" (John 17:16-20).

It will be noticed that the Lord prays to the Father "Sanctify them," that "they might be sanctified through the truth."

The apostle had learned the truth as it is in Jesus, and he says to the disciples in the church at Thessalonica:

"But we are bound to give thanks always to God for you, brethren beloved of the Lord, because God hath from the beginning chosen you to salvation through sanctification of the Spirit and belief of the truth: whereunto he called you by our gospel, to the obtaining of the glory of our Lord Jesus Christ" (2 Thessalonians 2:13, 14).

"Christ also loved the church, and gave himself for it; that he might sanctify and cleanse it with the washing of water by the word. That he might present it to himself a glorious church, not having spot, or wrinkle, or any such thing; but that it should be holy and without blemish" (Ephesians 5:25-27).

In view of the fact that without sanctification, or holiness, there is no salvation, the exhortations that abound in the Sacred Scriptures are worthy of earnest heed. The earnestness also with which the Lord prayed for the sanctification of his people should stir in the heart of each one an earnest resolve to watch against the approaches of sin, to resist the tempter, and to make unceasing prayer for the presence of the Holy Spirit. Not unnecessarily were the injunction and warning given:

"Follow peace with all men, and holiness, without which no man shall see the Lord: looking diligently lest any man fail of the grace of God" (Hebrews 12:14, 15).

"For the grace of God that bringeth salvation hath appeared to all men, Teaching us that, denying ungodliness and worldly lusts, we should live soberly, righteously, and godly, in this present world; looking for that blessed hope, and the glorious appearing of the great God and our Saviour Jesus Christ; who gave himself for us, that he might redeem us from all iniquity, and purify unto himself a peculiar people, zealous of good works" (Titus 2:11–14).

(7) The preservation of the saints

This subject is often called "The Perseverance of the Saints." The word "preservation," however, seems preferable, because it draws the attention directly to God, who is the Preserver of his people. The word "perseverance," on the other hand, points to the course of the believer, which is the direct result of the preserving power and grace of God. The doctrine of "the perseverance of the saints" can only be proved by bringing out those passages from the Scriptures which teach God's distinct purpose in regard to his own "preservation of the saints."

The all-important thing is then to get clear views of God's own gracious and unalterable purpose. We have already considered this purpose of God, by which he chose certain persons to inherit the kingdom prepared for them from the foundation of the world. The subject now before us is the carrying out of that purpose. The Apostle Paul gives us information on that subject:

"And we know that all things work together for good to them that love God, to them who are the called according to *his* purpose. For whom he did foreknow, he also did predestinate *to be* conformed to the image of his Son, that he might be the firstborn among many brethren. Moreover, whom he did predestinate, them he also called: and whom he called, them he also justified: and whom he justified, them he also glorified" (Romans 8:28–30).

Here is the purpose and the successive steps by which it is carried out; they are chosen, called, justified, glorified:

"Elect according to the foreknowledge of God the Father, through sanctification of the Spirit, unto obedience and sprinkling of the blood of Jesus Christ: Grace unto you, and peace, be multiplied. Blessed *be* the God and Father of our Lord Jesus Christ, which according to his abundant mercy hath begotten us again unto a lively hope by the resurrection of Jesus Christ from the dead. To an inheritance incorruptible, and undefiled, and that fadeth not away, reserved in heaven for you, who are kept by the power of God through faith unto salvation ready to be revealed in the last time" (1 Peter 1:2–5).

"Grace *be* unto you, and peace, from God our Father, and *from* the Lord Jesus Christ. I thank my God always on your behalf, for the grace of God which is given you by Jesus Christ; that in every thing ye are enriched by him, in all utterance, and *in* all knowledge; even as the testimony of Christ was confirmed in you: so that ye come behind in no gift; waiting for the coming of our Lord Jesus Christ: who shall also confirm you unto the end, *that ye may be* blameless in the day of our Lord Jesus Christ. God *is* faithful, by whom ye were called unto the fellowship of his Son Jesus Christ our Lord" (1 Corinthians 1:3–9).

These passages all point to the same truth, the confirming to the end of those who are "called into the fellowship of Jesus Christ our Lord," so that they "may be blameless in the day of our Lord Jesus Christ."

The Lord's sheep, whom the Father gave to him, he represents as being in his hands and in the hands of the Father, and gives the strongest assurance of their perfect safety there:

"My sheep hear my voice, and I know them, and they follow me: and I give unto them eternal life; and they shall never perish, neither shall any *man*, pluck them out of my hand. My Father, which gave *them* me, is greater than all; and no *man* is able to pluck *them* out of my Father's hand. I and my Father are one" (John 10:27–30).

In his effort to comfort his disciples, on the evening before his crucifixion, Jesus spoke to them words that come down through the ages, cheering his people in all generations:

"Let not your heart be troubled: ye believe in God, believe also in me. In my Father's house are many mansions: if *it were* not *so*, I would have told you. I go to prepare a place for you. And if I go and prepare a place for you, I will come again, and receive you unto myself; that where I am, *there* ye may be also" (John 14:1–3).

The object of God's electing grace will not be fully attained until those that the Father has given to the Son have been gathered into the bright mansions that have been prepared for them. Those that are the objects of God's preserving care can never fail to reach the desired end; for through the means which that loving care provides, they patiently persevere until they inherit the kingdom, and enter the royal mansions prepared for them in heaven. Hence, in the midst of the trials of life, and when passing through the valley of the shadow of death, they may sing joyfully, in the words of the poet Gambold:

"And when I'm to die,
'Receive me,' I'll cry;
      For Jesus has loved me, I cannot say why.
"But this I do find,
 We two are so joined
      He'll not live in glory and leave me behind."

6

How Christians Should Live and Labor

We have been considering what the Lord Jesus Christ has done for men while he dwelt on earth; we have also inquired what he has been doing, what he is now doing, and what he will continue to do for his followers until they are led up to heaven to be forever with him. We now come to ask what his people are to do day by day so long as they live in this world.

There are some things that ought to be clearly understood by each one of them, old and young, men and women. Let us try to learn from the Bible what it says about their daily life and their daily works. The Bible is given to us to teach us how to make the most of the short lives that we are to spend in this world.

"What! know ye not that your body is the temple of the Holy Ghost *which is in you*, which ye have of God, and ye are not your own! For ye are bought with a price: therefore glorify God in your body, and in your sprit, which are God's" (1 Corinthians 6:19, 20).

This passage tells us that the believer in Christ is not his own. Most of the followers of Christ have known and felt this to be true; but it ought never to be forgotten. They have often sung the words of that familiar hymn, beginning with the words:

> *"Alas! and did my Saviour bleed?*
> *And did my Sovereign die?*
> *Would he devote that sacred head*
> *For such a worm as I?"*

The last words of the hymn are generally sung with very deep feeling:

> *"But drops of grief can ne'er repay*
>   *The debt of love I owe;*
> *Here, Lord, I give myself away,*
>   *'Tis all that I can do."*

This means that they do not want to be their own, but really desire to belong now and forever to Christ; that they are glad to take him for their Lord and Master, and are ready to spend and be spent in his service. The faithful servant will, of course, be found asking day by day, "Lord, what wilt thou have me to do?" He should always remember that he will most glorify God by doing promptly, diligently, and faithfully what God wants him to do.

(1) It is the will of their Lord that, without any unnecessary delay, they shall be baptized in the name of the Father, and the Son, and the Holy Spirit.

It is not left to their choice whether they shall be baptized or not. How was it with those that were led to Christ by the preaching of the apostles? They were baptized at once. On the day of Pentecost, after the preaching of Peter, we read:

"Then they that gladly received his word were baptized: and the same day there were added *unto them* about three thousand souls. And they continued steadfastly in the apostles' doctrine and fellowship, and in breaking of bread, and in prayers" (Acts 2:41, 42).

Then, when Philip went down and preached at the city of Samaria, we find that believers were quickly baptized.

"But when they believed Philip preaching the things concerning the kingdom of God, and the name of Jesus Christ, they were baptized, both men and women" (Acts 8:12).

After this he preached Jesus to the eunuch of the queen of Ethiopia:

"And as they went on *their* way, they came unto a certain water: and the eunuch said, See, *here is* water; what doth hinder me to be baptized? And Philip said, If thou believest with all thine heart, thou mayest. And he answered and said, I believe that Jesus Christ is the Son of God. And he commanded the chariot to stand still: and they went down both into the water, both Philip and the eunuch; and he baptized him. And when they were come up out of the water, the Spirit of the Lord caught away Philip, that the eunuch saw him no more: and he went on his way rejoicing. But Philip was found at Azotus: and passing through he preached in all the cities, till he came to Cesarea" (Acts 8:36–40).

The baptism of Lydia at Philippi was immediately after "the Lord opened her heart, that she attended unto the things that were spoken by Paul" (Acts 16:14, 15). The apostle acted according to the command of the Lord, and was evidently prompt in speaking to her of baptism and in administering the ordinance.

So also with the jailer at Philippi. At midnight in the prison Paul and Silas preached Jesus unto him:

"Then he called for a light, and sprang in, and came trembling, and fell down before Paul and Silas, and brought them out, and said, Sirs, what must I do to be saved? And they said, Believe on the Lord Jesus Christ, and thou shalt be saved, and thy house. And they spake unto him the word of the Lord, and to all that were in his house. And he took them the same hour of the night, and washed *their* stripes; and was baptized, he and all his, straightway. And when he had brought them into his house, he set meat before them, and rejoiced, believing in God with all his house" (Acts 16:29–34).

These instances of apostolic practice show that the apostles and early Christians faithfully taught this command of Christ, and everywhere promptly obeyed it.

These passages also show us what the act of baptism was. Philip and the eunuch "went down both into the water; and he baptized him"; then they came "up out of the water," the command having been obeyed. In a similar way we read (Matthew 3:16) that "Jesus, when he was baptized, went up straightway out of the water," the Lord having submitted to the ordinance just as God had given it to John. John and Paul and Philip would not have made any change. Certainly the Lord would not have consented to submit to anything different from what was commanded.

There is in the minds of many a very mistaken idea of what real, honest obedience to the command of the Lord means. It was very aptly illustrated by a faithful, but uneducated man some years ago. He was a laboring man, and was one day working for a prominent physician. During the day the physician, a Pedobaptist, entered into conversation with him, and after a time turned to the subject of baptism. At length he said:

"I do not see the use of being so particular about it; it makes no difference whether one is baptized in the ocean, or has a few drops of water sprinkled on his forehead. One is just as good as the other."

"I don't see that," said the simple-hearted man. "It seems to me that it makes a great difference whether we obey or whether we don't obey. Suppose you tell me to go down to the market, and get you a bushel of turnips. Then suppose I think that a bushel of potatoes is as good as a bushel of turnips, and so I fetch you potatoes, because it makes no difference. Would you think I obeyed you? Wouldn't you tell me to take them right back, and fetch what you told me to fetch? It seems to me that if we really want to obey the Lord, we ought to try to do just exactly what he tells us. I'd be ashamed to fetch you what you did not want, just as if I was bringing what you told me to get, and then tell you it made no difference. And just so, if I had been only sprinkled instead of being baptized just like Jesus was, I'd be ashamed to go up and tell the Lord that it didn't make any difference."

This poor man had the real spirit of obedience—a desire and design to do just exactly what he tells us. That is what all of the disciples of Christ should do. He himself went down into the water and was baptized, and came up out of the water. The disciples are to be "followers"—that is, *imitators*, of their Lord. They are to be,

"Buried with him in baptism" (Colossians 2:12).

"Know ye not, that so many of us as were baptized into Jesus Christ were baptized into his death? Therefore we are buried with him by baptism into death; that like as Christ was raised up from the dead by the glory of the Father, even so we also should walk in newness of life" (Romans 6:3, 4).

When all believers in Christ really and cheerfully obey him in this matter, doing "just exactly what he tells us," then there will be a great step taken toward that "Christian Union," of which so much is said in these days.

(2) THEY ARE TO UNITE THEMSELVES IN CHURCH FELLOWSHIP WITH SUCH OTHER BELIEVERS AS TEACH AND OBSERVE ALL THE COMMANDMENTS AND ORDINANCES OF THE GOSPEL.

The Scriptures show that this church fellowship was in accord with the will of God.

"Then they that gladly received his word were baptized: and the same day there were added *unto them* about three thousand souls. And they continued steadfastly in the apostle's doctrine and fellowship, and in breaking of bread, and in prayers" (Acts 2:41, 42).

"Neither pray I for these alone, but for them also which shall believe on me through their word; that they all may be one; as thou, Father, *art* in me, and I in thee, that they also may be one in us: that the world may believe that thou hast sent me" (John 17:20, 21).

"And *this they did*, not as we hoped, but first gave their own selves to the Lord, and unto us by the will of God" (2 Corinthians 8:5).

"Even so ye, forasmuch as ye are zealous of spiritual *gifts*, seek that ye may excel to the edifying of the church" (1 Corinthians 14:12).

The very nature of the case makes it both needful and natural for believers to unite themselves in churches. They are of one family, of one mind, of one spirit, of one hope. The world, the flesh, and the devil are against them all alike. Hence, oneness of spirit, of character, and of purpose show not only the possibility of union, sympathy, and co-operation, but also the need for these Christian virtues. By unity the saints are strengthened, comforted, instructed, and edified.

(3) THE CHURCHES COMPOSED OF BELIEVERS WHO HAVE BEEN BAPTIZED IN OBEDIENCE TO THE LORD'S COMMAND AND AFTER HIS EXAMPLE ARE TO OBSERVE THE LORD'S SUPPER, THE ORDINANCE THAT HE INSTITUTED TO COMMEMORATE HIS DEATH.

"And as they were eating, Jesus took bread, and blessed *it*, and brake *it*, and gave *it* to the disciples, and said, Take, eat; this is my body. And he took the cup, and gave thanks, and gave it to them, saying, Drink ye all of it; for this is my blood of the new testament, which is shed for many for the remission of sins. But I say unto you, I will not drink henceforth of this fruit of the vine, until that day when I drink it new with you in my Father's kingdom" (Matthew 26:26–29).

"And he took bread, and gave thanks, and brake *it*, and gave unto them, saying, This is my body which is given for you: this do in remembrance of me. Likewise also the cup after supper, saying, This cup is the new testament in my blood, which is shed for you" (Luke 22:19, 20).

The ordinance was faithfully observed and handed down by the apostles:

"For I have received of the Lord that which also I delivered unto you. That the Lord Jesus, the *same* night in which he was betrayed, took bread: and when he had given thanks, he brake it, and said, Take, eat; this is my body, which is broken for you: this do in remembrance of me. After the same manner also he took the cup when he had supped, saying, This cup is the new testament in my blood: this do ye, as oft as ye drink it, in remembrance of me. For as often as ye eat this bread, and drink this cup, ye do shew the Lord's death till he come" (1 Corinthians 11:23–26).

"The cup of blessing which we bless, is it not a participation of the blood of Christ? The bread which we break, is it not a participation of the body of Christ?" (1 Corinthians 10:16, Revised Version).

(4) THEY ARE TO STRIVE TO EDIFY ONE ANOTHER, AND THUS BUILD UP AND STRENGTHEN THE CHURCH.

In the New Testament the word edify is full of meaning. The church of Christ is represented as a building, as when the Lord says to Simon Peter:

"And I say also unto thee, That thou art Peter, and upon this rock I will build my church; and the gates of hell shall not prevail against it" (Matthew 16:18).

Again the Apostle Paul refers to the church, or "the body of Christ," as a building. He says:

"But unto every one of us is given grace according to the measure of the gift of Christ. Wherefore he saith, When he ascended up on high, he led captivity captive, and gave gifts unto men. ... And he gave some, apostles; and some, prophets; and some, evangelists; and some, pastors and teachers; for the perfecting of the saints, for the work of the ministry, for the edifying [or, building up] of the body of Christ" (Ephesians 4:7, 8, 11, 12).

It is here stated that upon "every one of us"—that is, on all the members of "the body of Christ," Christ has conferred some gift that is profitable for the building up of the church. This is his "house."

"That thou mayest know how thou oughtest to behave thyself in the house of God, which is the church of the living God" (1 Timothy 3:15).

"Ye also, as lively stones, are built up a spiritual house" (1 Peter 2:5).

"Christ as a Son over his own house, whose house are we" (Hebrews 3:6).

"Know ye not that ye are the temple of God, and that the Spirit of God dwelleth in you? If any man defile the temple of God him shall God destroy; for the temple of God is holy, which temple ye are" (1 Corinthians 3:16, 17).

This church, this house, this temple of God, is to be built up, and "every one of us" has received some gift to fit him for a helper in the building up. "Those who by action, instruction, exhortation, comfort, promote the Christian wisdom of others, and help them to live a correspondent life, are regarded as taking part in the erection of that building [that is, the church, or temple of God, in which the Holy Spirit dwells]; and hence are said to edify, *to promote growth in Christian wisdom, affection, grace, virtue, holiness, blessedness.*"

What a glorious work that building, that house of God, that temple, that church will be when finished! And what a blessed privilege it is that "every one of us," as the apostle says, has some gift from Christ to fit him for helping on its completion! Let every one keep fixed in mind the thought, "I am called by the blessed Jesus to help in building up his glorious house," and seek daily grace and help, so that he may build wisely and rapidly!

(5) THEY ARE TO DO ALL THAT LIES IN THEIR POWER TO TEACH, OR MAKE DISCIPLES OF, ALL NATIONS ACCORDING TO THE LORD'S GREAT COMMISSION.

As there is no one that cannot do something for the building up of the church, the house of God, so there is no one that is not able to help in some way in making the gospel known throughout all the world. The Lord has a work for the young as well as the old, for the weak as well as the strong. It was a little Jewish girl that was the means of pointing Naaman, the captain of the hosts of the King of Syria, to means by which he was cured of the deadly leprosy. And often, in the gathering of sinners to the feet of Jesus the Saviour, that saying has been fulfilled: "A little child shall lead them."

One thing should be borne in mind, that we are not to try to decide what are little and what are great things in work for the salvation of men. A thing may seem to be little, but in the course of time it may lead on to very great results. The Christian worker must learn to "despise not the day of small things." There is one thought that may be useful to those who do not think they have a gift for doing great things. Such an one, when he has done the thing that God has laid before him, has finished the work that was given to him, and those who finish their work shall not lose their reward.

Private conversation with kinsmen, friends, neighbors, and strangers, as opportunity may offer, is an important means of grace. It is well to resolve never to permit a suitable opportunity to pass unimproved or unused, lest we should become guilty of the blood of our fellow-men and of unfaithfulness to our Lord.

But one who is seeking faithfully to be a follower, or imitator, of Christ will not be satisfied with using opportunities that are thrown from time to time in his way. Jesus came "to seek and to save the lost." This means much more than trying to save those that we may "chance to meet," as we say. It is one thing to meet some one, and then use the opportunity to speak to him of Jesus and his salvation; it is a different thing to think first of some one and then seek for an opportunity to present to him the great salvation and urge him to accept it. Jesus sought the lost; he did not sit down at ease, and wait for them to seek him. Christians are accustomed to sing with great thankfulness:

> "Jesus sought me when a stranger,
> Wandering from the fold of God."

They very well know that he first sought them, and that, had he not done so, they never would have been brought into his blessed fold. It is as seekers for the lost that the followers of Christ and his churches will be most blessed in becoming the instruments of saving them. "He that winneth souls is wise," says Solomon (Proverbs 11:30), and those that, like their Lord, seek souls will exercise true wisdom and reap its rich rewards.

We have a beautiful example of this kind of work in the Gospel of John:

"One of the two which heard John *speak,* and followed him, was Andrew, Simon Peter's brother. He first findeth his own brother Simon, and saith unto him, We have found the Messias, which is, being interpreted, the Christ. And he brought him to Jesus. And when Jesus beheld him, he said, Thou art Simon the son of Jona: thou shalt be called Cephas, which is by interpretation, A stone.

"The day following Jesus would go forth into Galilee, and findeth Philip, and saith unto him, Follow me. Now Philip was of Bethsaida, the city of Andrew and Peter. Philip findeth Nathanael, and saith unto him, We have found him, of whom Moses in the law, and the prophets, did write, Jesus of Nazareth, the son of Joseph. And Nathanael said unto him, Can there any good thing come out of Nazareth? Philip saith unto him, Come and see. Jesus saw Nathanael coming to him, and saith of him, Behold an Israelite indeed, in whom is no guile! Nathanael saith unto him, Whence knowest thou me? Jesus answered and said unto him, Before that Philip called thee, when thou wast under the fig tree, I saw thee. Nathanael answered and saith unto him, Rabbi, thou art the Son of God; thou art the King of Israel" (John 1:40-49).

Their joy was so great because they had been brought to know Christ, that they sought to make others know him also. Their words were blessed. Nearly three thousand years ago the power of fitting words was well known, as the following passages will show:

"A man hath joy by the answer of his mouth: and a word *spoken* in due season, how good *is it!*" (Proverbs 15:23).

"A word fitly spoken *is like* apples of gold in pictures of silver" (Proverbs 25:11).

One who has a heart for this sort of work, who is desirous to imitate Jesus in this important part of his work, will find or make abundant opportunity for sowing good seed, whose fruitfulness will be both sure and abundant. The wise and faithful words of Nathan the prophet were the means of leading David to deep repentance and to humble confession of his great sin. He sought out the royal transgressor, and addressed him in bold and stern words:

"Thou art the man. ... Wherefore hast thou despised the commandment of the Lord to do evil in his sight. ... And David said unto Nathan, I have sinned against the Lord" (2 Samuel 12:7, 9, 13).

These plain, brave, and stern words ground David as the millstones grind the wheat. For months he seems to have been untroubled by the remembrance of his great crime, and there was great need that he should be sought. He was at once brought to see and to feel and to confess his guilt; and in the Fifty-first Psalm he expresses his sorrow for his sin, his sense of it as a sin against God, his desire for a clean heart and a right spirit, and the restoration of the joy of salvation; then he adds:

"Then will I teach transgressors thy ways; and sinners shall be converted unto thee" (Psalm 51:13).

In every generation, from that day to our own, has he been teaching the ways of God, and aiding transgressors to draw near to him with deep contrition, yet with humble trust.

(6) THEY ARE TO DO GOOD BY A PURE AND SPOTLESS CHRISTIAN LIFE.

The Lord laid great stress on the power for good that his people were to exert by the spirit that they manifested, the words that they spoke, and the daily and hourly influence of their life and conversation in the world.

In the Sermon on the Mount, Jesus points out a number of things that should appear in the ordinary life of his disciples:

"Blessed are the poor in spirit." These are such as are aware of their own spiritual poverty and imperfection, and humbly look to God for a supply to meet their spiritual wants. The "poor in spirit" are like the publican who had a deep sense of his own sinfulness and prayed, "God be merciful to me a sinner." He was the very opposite of the Pharisee who was puffed up because he thought himself to be so very unlike other men, so different from the poor publican that stood near him.

"Blessed are the meek." Those that have that quiet and unassuming spirit that was so manifest in the life of the Lord Jesus. It is well described in the words of the Apostle Paul when writing of charity:

"Charity [or, 'love'] suffereth long, and is kind; charity envieth not; charity vaunteth not itself, is not puffed up, doth not behave itself unseemly, seeketh not her own, is not easily provoked" (1 Corinthians 13:4, 5).

"Blessed are the merciful." Not only those who seek to be kind even when they have to be strictly just in dealing with the guilty, but those who care for the suffering and the needy.

"Blessed are the pure in heart." Those whose thoughts delight to dwell on the holiness of God and heaven, and who do not cherish wicked, filthy, degrading thoughts and purposes in their hearts.

"Blessed are the peacemakers." There are persons who seem to walk through the world day by day, always finding somebody or something to rouse their angry feelings, and always, by emphatic expression of their angry feelings, stirring up discord and strife as they pass along. There are others who seem to bear about with them an atmosphere of calmness and tranquillity. If they come into the midst of a tumultuous company of angry people, the tones of their voice as they speak and the words that they utter seem to act on the excited people as oil on the troubled waves; they soon sink down, and there is a great calm.

"Blessed" are those who walk, like angels from the peaceful presence of God, along life's pathway, neither by word nor act rousing up strife and contention, but whose very presence has power to hush the tumult of angry voices and bring in the sweet calm of peace! Thrice blessed those who lead men of carnal hearts, full of enmity to God and his Christ, to see the wickedness and folly of their course, and to come to the feet of Jesus confessing their sin! Thus they become peacemakers indeed, the instruments in God's hands of making men partakers of the peace of God which passeth all understanding!

In the passages just quoted, Jesus refers to the spirit and temper of his people, and the manner in which they walk in the midst of others in this wicked world. He then proceeds to speak of the true position that they hold in the wicked world where they are left for a season:

"Ye are the salt of the earth: but if the salt have lost his savour, wherewith shall it be salted? it is thenceforth good for nothing, but to be cast out, and to be trodden under foot of men" (Matthew 5:13).

"Ye are the salt of the earth." That is, they are in a world where corruption abounds, and the natural tendency of corruption is to spread and increase until corruption ends in death. But they are the salt of the earth, continued here in God's benevolent design as a preservative power, in order to prevent the spread of corruption and the speedy coming of the sad end toward which unchecked corruption hurries men.

"Ye are the light of the world." One of the familiar terms by which the Scriptures represent the condition of the worldly man is to say that they sit or walk in darkness. The works of wicked men are "unfruitful works of darkness"; they themselves are under "the power of darkness"; they are "in darkness"; they walk in darkness, and darkness hath blinded their eyes; they "love darkness rather than light, because their deeds are evil." They "sit in darkness and the shadow of death."

The Lord, however, puts his people in strong contrast with the men of the world. They are "the light of the world." They are not the light in the same sense as the Lord himself. He, as the Son of God, "is light, and in him is no darkness at all." They are light, because they are enlightened by their Lord in order that they may shed light on the darkness of the world while he is withdrawn. It was his design in leaving them here in this dark and evil world, that they should be seen, like a bright light flashing forth on the darkness. No man lights a lamp to put it under a bushel; it was meant to be placed where men could see it. Therefore the Lord lays a solemn command on them:

"Let your light so shine before men that they may see your good works, and glorify your Father which is in heaven" (Matthew 5:16).

All the graces that he had mentioned before should be earnestly cultivated. Their spirit, their words, and their actions should be in such strong contrast with the works of the children of darkness, that these darkened ones may be convinced of their sin and made to feel their need, and be prepared to call earnestly upon Jesus to forgive their sins and help them to become lights also. The disciples of Christ should clearly understand that every sin, in thought, in word, in action, dims their light, and unfits them for the blessed work to which their Lord calls them. Alas, for those who for want of watchfulness and prayer thus lose their spiritual power, and leave those about them to perish in their darkness!

(7) THEY ARE TO PRAY THAT LABORERS MAY BE SENT INTO THE HARVEST FIELD, AND THAT THE BLESSING OF GOD MAY REST ABUNDANTLY ON THEIR LABORS.

In the days of his own labors on earth the Lord had given special instruction and exhortation on this subject to his disciples:

"But when he saw the multitudes, he was moved with compassion on them, because they fainted, and were scattered abroad, as sheep having no shepherd. Then saith he unto his disciples, The harvest truly *is* plenteous, but the labourers are few; pray ye therefore the Lord of the harvest, that he will send forth labourers into his harvest" (Matthew 9:36–38).

"Say not ye, There are yet four months, and *then* cometh harvest? behold, I say unto you, Lift up your eyes, and look on the fields; for they are white already to harvest. And he that reapeth receiveth wages, and gathereth fruit unto life eternal: that both he that soweth and he that reapeth may rejoice together" (John 4:35, 36).

The disciples probably retained a lively recollection of these words of their Lord. For we read that after he had given to them his direction to go into all the world, he also,

"Commanded them that they should not depart from Jerusalem, but wait for the promise of the Father, which, saith he, ye have heard of me. ... But ye shall receive power, after that the Holy Ghost is come upon you: and ye shall be witnesses unto me both in Jerusalem, and in all Judea, and in Samaria, and unto the uttermost part of the earth" (Acts 1:4, 8).

After giving this command and the subsequent promise, the Lord ascended to heaven.

"Then returned they unto Jerusalem, from the mount called Olivet, which is from Jerusalem a sabbath day's journey. And when they were come in, they went up into an upper room, where abode both Peter, and James, and John, and Andrew, Philip, and Thomas, Bartholomew, and Matthew, James *the son* of Alpheus, and Simon Zelotes, and Judas *the brother* of James. These all continued with one accord in prayer and supplication, with the women, and Mary the mother of Jesus, and with his brethren" (Acts 1:12-14).

After some days of prayer by the disciples, the expected answer came:

"And when the day of Pentecost was fully come, they were all with one accord in one place. And suddenly there came a sound from heaven as of a rushing mighty wind, and it filled all the house where they were sitting. And there appeared unto them cloven tongues like as of fire, and it sat upon each of them. And they were all filled with the Holy Ghost, and began to speak with other tongues, as the Spirit gave them utterance. And there were dwelling at Jerusalem Jews, devout men, out of every nation under heaven.

"Now when this was noised abroad, the multitude came together, and were confounded, because that every man heard them speak in his own language. And they were all amazed and marvelled, saying one to another, Behold, are not all these which speak Galileans? And how hear we every man in our own tongue, wherein we were born? Parthians, and Medes, and Elamites, and the dwellers in Mesopotamia, and in Judea, and Cappadocia, in Pontus, and Asia, Phrygia, and Pamphylia, in Egypt, and in the parts of Libya about Cyrene, and strangers of Rome, Jews and proselytes, Cretes and Arabians, we do hear them speak in our tongues the wonderful works of God. And they were all amazed, and were in doubt, *saying* one to another, What meaneth this?" (Acts 2:1-12).

Thus we see that a copious effusion of the Holy Spirit was poured upon them, filling them with power and wisdom, and thus fitting them for effectual work in preaching the gospel. The gracious Lord who answered their prayer is ready to answer similar requests from all his obedient servants. The lack of earnest and believing prayer on the part of his churches is, no doubt, the cause of the spiritual unfruitfulness under which they sometimes groan. Were earnest and unceasing prayers ascending to the throne of grace for all of the messengers who preach the gospel in different lands throughout the world, we should no longer look out on parching fields and withering flowers, for the showers of heavenly grace would be constantly and abundantly descending, and the wide fields of the world would flourish like the garden of the Lord.

This same day three thousand converts were added to the church. What was the source of this wondrous display of power and grace? It was the coming of the Holy Spirit. To whom did he come with such matchless power? It was to a company of one hundred and twenty who had given themselves to earnest prayer for the bestowment of this inestimable gift. What wonders of power and grace may we not expect when with one accord the millions of believers in Christ throughout the world unite in earnest prayer to the God of all grace for a real Pentecostal season to be enjoyed by every nation and kindred and people and tongue under the whole heaven?

(8) THEY ARE TO GIVE OF THEIR MEANS AS GOD HAS PROSPERED THEM, FOR THE SUPPORT OF THOSE THAT GO OUT TO THE NATIONS TO CARRY TO THEM THE NEWS OF SALVATION IN CHRIST.

When the Lord gave his Great Commission to his disciples, the command was binding on them and on those who believed through their word; the work was wide, the nations were many and widely scattered. The Lord desired that all, even those the farthest from Jerusalem, should hear the gospel and believe and be baptized, and taught his holy will. It would need that many should go forth, giving themselves to the work, and need that those who did not go should be happy and honored sharers in the work, by praying for those who did go, and giving of their means to support them. He had himself gone forth in the same work, setting an example for those who should go out; for we read:

"And Jesus went about all the cities and villages, teaching in their synagogues, and preaching the gospel of the kingdom, and healing every sickness and every disease among the people" (Matthew 9:35).

His work was confined to the lost sheep of the house of Israel, but after his death and resurrection and ascension the tidings of salvation was to be carried everywhere.

"And he said unto them, Go ye into all the world, and preach the gospel to every creature. He that believeth and is baptized shall be saved; but he that believeth not shall be damned. And these signs shall follow them that believe; In my name shall they cast out devils; they shall speak with new tongues; they shall take up serpents; and if they drink any deadly thing, it shall not hurt them; they shall lay hands on the sick, and they shall recover. So then, after the Lord had spoken unto them, he was received up into heaven, and sat on the right hand of God. And they went forth, and preached every where, the Lord working with *them*, and confirming the word with signs following" (Mark 16:15–20).

The Lord's purpose and earnest desire looked to the seeking and saving of all the lost. He gave himself to this as his great life work, and never rested until he went up to enter on his mediatorial work in heaven. He thus set his followers an example, that they might see it and fashion their lives according to it. If they imitate his example, they show that they have his Spirit. If they do not imitate his example, it goes directly to show that they have not his Spirit; and to all such the words of the apostle should be the subject of very careful study:

"Now if *any man* have not the Spirit of Christ, he is none of his" (Romans 8:9).

Even under the Jewish Dispensation, the withholding of means for carrying forward the work of God was emphatically rebuked, and gracious promises given to those who gave as the Lord had prospered them:

"For I *am* the Lord, I change not; therefore ye sons of Jacob are not consumed. Even from the days of your fathers ye are gone away from mine ordinances, and have not kept *them*. Return unto me, and I will return unto you, saith the Lord of hosts. But ye said, Wherein shall we return? Will a man rob God? Yet ye have robbed me. But ye say, Wherein have we robbed thee? In tithes and offerings. Ye *are* cursed with a curse: for ye have robbed me, *even* this whole nation. Bring ye all the tithes into the storehouse, that there may be meat in mine house, and prove me now herewith, saith the Lord of hosts, if I will not open you the windows of heaven, and pour you out a blessing, that *there shall* not *be room* enough *to receive it*. And I will rebuke the devourer for your sakes, and he shall not destroy the fruits of your ground; neither shall your vine cast her fruit before the time in the field, saith the Lord of hosts. And all nations shall call you blessed: for ye shall be a delightsome land, saith the Lord of hosts" (Malachi 3:6–12; see Leviticus 27:30–34).

God complains here of the people of Israel, because though he had asked only one-tenth of what he had given them, they had robbed him of that. He encourages them to bring in his tithes, saying to them that if they will, he will open them the windows of heaven, and pour out such great blessings that they shall not have room to store them:

"Honour the Lord with thy substance, and with the firstfruits of all thine increase: so shall thy barns be filled with plenty, and thy presses shall burst out with new wine" (Proverbs 3:9, 10).

"Now concerning the collection for the saints, as I have given order to the churches of Galatia, even so do ye. Upon the first *day* of the week let every one of you lay by him in store, as *God* hath prospered him, that there be no gatherings when I come" (1 Corinthians 16:1, 2).

"Three times in a year shall all thy males appear before the Lord thy God in the place which he shall choose; in the feast of unleavened bread, and in the feast of weeks, and in the feast of tabernacles: and they shall not appear before the Lord empty: every man *shall give* as he is able, according to the blessing of the Lord thy God which he hath given thee" (Deuteronomy 16:16, 17).

God forbids empty-handed service. We can see why. First, lip service costs nothing, and hence it does not prove the heart. Second, it does nothing to deny and crucify self. The giving of our wealth, if it be true giving, is the giving of ourselves. This ought to be deliberately done. It should never be forgotten that we are not our own—we are the Lord's: First, because he made us; we did not make ourselves; soul and body, mind and muscle, are from him. Second, he has preserved us alive. From him have come each breath, each ray of sunshine, each shower. From his hand come the flowing streams and the fruitful fields. Third, he has redeemed us from death and hell, having given himself a ransom for us. The world, with all its treasures of gold, of silver, of rivers and of plains, is his. We are his creatures, occupying his creation. Hence, it is plain that we cannot occupy upon our own terms. We are only as tenants, tarrying temporarily and occupying conditionally.

Moreover, the kingdom of grace of which we are subjects—if we are saved instead of lost—needs to be supported. At present the kingdom tarries; it camps amid the forms and scenes of matter, and while it thus camps it will always have need of material aid in carrying on its work; that is to say, it must have money, horses, cars, ships, bread, clothes, men, and women. Who shall supply these if not the subjects of the kingdom? Are not people under the governments of this world willing to be taxed for the support of their governments? Can it be that those who are so favored as to be subjects of the kingdom of heaven are less willing to contribute for the support and extension of that glorious kingdom?

Then, our Lord so loved men that he gave himself to save them. Can we spurn or neglect the work he loved so dearly? Who but the churches shall send and publish this word of reconciliation to souls still in rebellion? Has hell no terrors, and heaven no joys? Believers should be incited to cheerful and liberal giving, for:

"God so loved the world that he gave his only begotten Son, that whosoever believeth in him should not perish, but have everlasting life" (John 3:16).

"Christ also loved the church, and gave himself for it" (Ephesians 5:25).

God the Holy Spirit is here, having been sent down on this same mission of grace. The angels are ministering spirits sent forth to minister to them who shall be heirs of salvation. Prophets and apostles, kings and priests, have set their hearts on the world's redemption, even unto the sacrifice of all on earth.

The glory of the object to be obtained by the furtherance of the gospel should also stimulate them. The money given goes to save souls from the outer darkness and the regions of despair. It goes to spread the knowledge of the Lord, to restore men to that law that is holy, just, and good. It goes forth to dislodge Satan, and to blot out sin and misery. It goes to bring glory to God, honor to Christ, and to make peace and good will among men. What believer is that who is too indifferent, too blind, too cold, to be influenced by such considerations, to give of his means as God has prospered him, in order to further the testimony of the gospel? Oh, that men might be led to bring all their tobacco money, their whiskey money, and the money spent for gluttony and needless dress, and lay it down at Jesus' feet!

(9) They are to cherish in their hearts, and to manifest in their love, fervent love to God and one another.

It is to be feared that the cultivation of love in the heart does not command as it should the earnest and constant efforts of the followers of Christ. It is, however, that grace which should be cultivated with special earnestness. The Apostle Paul exhorts the Corinthians: "Covet earnestly the best gifts; and yet I shew unto you a more excellent way" (1 Corinthians 12:31).

Then he proceeds to point out in very impressive words the real importance of love:

"Though I speak with the tongues of men and of angels, and have not charity [that is, *love*], I am become *as* sounding brass, or a tinkling cymbal. And though I have *the gift of* prophecy, and understand all mysteries, and all knowledge; and though I have all faith, so that I could remove mountains, and have not charity, I am nothing. And though I bestow all my goods to feed *the poor*, and though I give my body to be burned, and have not charity, it profiteth me nothing" (1 Corinthians 13:1–3).

The Lord, when questioned as to the most important of the commands of God, gave his testimony as to the prominence that belongs to love in the Christian character and life:

"And one of the scribes came, and having heard them reasoning together, and perceiving that he had answered them well, asked him, Which is the first commandment of all? And Jesus answered him, The first of all the commandments is, Hear, O Israel; The Lord our God is one Lord: and thou shalt love the Lord thy God with all thy heart, and with all thy soul, and with all thy mind, and with all thy strength: this *is* the first commandment. And the second *is* like, *namely* this, Thou shalt love thy neighbour as thyself. There is none other commandment greater than these. And the scribe said unto him, Well, Master, thou hast said the truth: for there is one God; and there is none other but he: and to love him with all the heart, and with all the understanding, and with all the soul, and with all the strength, and to love *his* neighbour as himself, is more than all whole burnt offerings and sacrifices. And when Jesus saw that he answered discreetly, he said unto him, Thou art not far from the kingdom of God. And no man after that durst ask him *any question*" (Mark 12:28–34).

This subject of love to God, of love to his people, and of love that goes out as did the love of Christ toward all men, even toward enemies, is of such importance that it calls for more full consideration. Let us present some other statements, that were made by the Lord, by Paul, by Peter, by John:

"A new commandment I give unto you, That ye love one another; as I have loved you, that ye also love one another. By this shall all *men* know that ye are my disciples, if *ye* have love one to another" (John 13:34, 35).

"If ye love me, keep my commandments" (John 14:15).

"He that hath my commandments, and keepeth them, he it is that loveth me: and he that loveth me shall be loved of my Father, and I will love him, and will manifest myself to him. Judas saith unto him, not Iscariot, Lord, how is it that thou will manifest thyself unto us, and not unto the world? Jesus answered and said unto him, If a man love me, he will keep my words: and my Father will love him, and we will come unto him, and make our abode with him. He that loveth me not keepeth not my sayings: and the word which ye hear is not mine, but the Father's which sent me" (John 14:21–24).

"As the Father hath loved me, so have I loved you: continue ye in my love. If ye keep my commandments, ye shall abide in my love; even as I have kept my Father's commandments, and abide in his love. This is my commandment, That ye love one another, as I have loved you. Greater love hath no man than this, that a man lay down his life for his friends. Ye are my friends, if ye do whatsoever I command you. Henceforth I call you not servants; for the servant knoweth not what his lord doeth: but I have called you friends; for all things that I have heard of my Father I have made known unto you. These things I command you, that ye love one another. If the world hate you, ye know that it hated me before *it hated* you. If ye were of the world, the world would love his own; but because ye are not of the world, but I have chosen you out of the world, therefore the world hateth you" (John 15:9, 10, 12–15, 17–19).

"*Let* love be without dissimulation. Abhor that which is evil; cleave to that which is good. *Be* kindly affectioned one to another with brotherly love; in honour preferring one another" (Romans 12:9, 10).

"Render therefore to all their dues: tribute to whom tribute *is* due; custom to whom custom; fear to whom fear; honour to whom honour. Owe no man any thing, but to love one another: for he that loveth another hath fulfilled the law. For this, Thou shalt not commit adultery, Thou shalt not kill, Thou shalt not steal, Thou shalt not bear false witness, Thou shalt not covet; and if *there be* any other commandment, it is briefly comprehended in this saying, namely Thou shalt love thy neighbour as thyself: Love worketh no ill to his neighbour: therefore love *is* the fulfilling of the law" (Romans 13:8–10).

"Seeing ye have purified your souls in obeying the truth through the Spirit unto unfeigned love of the brethren, *see that ye* love one another with a pure heart fervently: being born again, not of corruptible seed, but of incorruptible, by the word of God, which liveth and abideth for ever" (1 Peter 1:22, 23).

"And above all things have fervent charity among yourselves: for charity shall cover the multitude of sins" (1 Peter 4:8).

"And besides this, giving all diligence, add to your faith virtue; and to virtue, knowledge; and to knowledge, temperance; and to temperance, patience; and to patience, godliness; and to godliness, brotherly kindness; and to brotherly kindness, charity. For if these things be in you, and abound, they make *you that ye shall* neither *be* barren nor unfruitful in the knowledge of our Lord

Jesus Christ. But he that lacketh these things is blind, and cannot see afar off, and hath forgotten that he was purged from his old sins. Wherefore the rather, brethren, give diligence to make your calling and election sure: for if ye do these things, ye shall never fall: for so an entrance shall be ministered unto you abundantly into the everlasting kingdom of our Lord and Saviour Jesus Christ" (2 Peter 1:5–11).

"And hereby we do know that we know him, if we keep his commandments. He that saith, I know him, and keepeth not his commandments, is a liar, and the truth is not in him. But whoso keepeth his word, in him verily is the love of God perfected: hereby know we that we are in him. He that saith he abideth in him ought himself also so to walk, even as he walked. Brethren, I write no new commandment unto you, but an old commandment which ye had from the beginning. The old commandment is the word which ye have heard from the beginning. Again, a new commandment I write unto you, which thing is true in him and in you: because the darkness is past, and the true light now shineth. He that saith he is in the light, and hateth his brother, is in darkness even until now. He that loveth his brother abideth in the light, and there is none occasion of stumbling in him. But he that hateth his brother is in darkness, and walketh in darkness, and knoweth not whither he goeth, because that darkness hath blinded his eyes" (1 John 2:3–11).

"In this the children of God are manifest, and the children of the devil: whosoever doeth not righteousness is not of God, neither he that loveth not his brother. For this is the message that ye heard from the beginning, that we should love one another. Not as Cain, *who* was of that wicked one, and slew his brother. And wherefore slew he him? Because his own works were evil, and his brother's righteous. Marvel not, my brethren, if the world hate you. We know that we have passed from death unto life, because we love the brethren. He that loveth not *his* brother abideth in death. Whosoever hateth his brother is a murderer: and ye know that no murderer hath eternal life abiding in him. Hereby perceive we the love *of God,* because he laid down his life for us: and we ought to lay down *our* lives for the brethren. But whoso hath this world's good, and seeth his brother have need, and shutteth up his bowels *of compassion* from him, how dwelleth the love of God in him? My little children, let us not love in word, neither in tongue; but in deed and in truth. And hereby we know that we are of the truth, and shall assure our hearts before him" (1 John 3:10–19).

"Beloved, let us love one another: for love is of God; and every one that loveth is born of God, and knoweth God. He that loveth not, knoweth not God; for God is love. In this was manifested the love of God toward us, because that God sent his only begotten Son into the world, that we might live through him. Herein is love, not that we loved God, but that he loved us, and sent his Son *to be* the propitiation for our sins. Beloved, if God so loved us, we ought also to love one another. No man hath seen God at any time. If we love one another, God dwelleth in us, and his love is perfected in us" (1 John 4:7-12).

"Whosoever believeth that Jesus is the Christ is born of God: and every one that loveth him that begat, loveth him also that is begotten of him. By this we know that we love the children of God, when we love God, and keep his commandments. For this is the love of God, that we keep his commandments: and his commandments are not grievous" (1 John 5:13).

There *are* two things brought out distinctly in these passages. First, that love to God and love to our neighbors should be cultivated by the believer in Christ with the deepest earnestness. "God is love," and those who desire to grow into the likeness of their Heavenly Father should prayerfully and earnestly seek for such an increase of love that they may come, as the Lord expresses it, to "love the Lord thy God with all thy heart, and with all thy soul, and with all thy mind, and with all thy strength"; and to "love thy neighbour as thyself," and to develop a love for their brethren such as Jesus describes in his new commandment, "that ye love one another; as I have loved you, that ye also love another." This is the standard which the Lord sets up before those whom he has loved, and for whom he has given himself. It was designed that it should be studied, and that each believer should carefully test himself by it, and never rest satisfied until, by the aid of the Holy Spirit, conformity to it has been attained. The high and holy standard should be kept continually in full view, until,

"We all with open face beholding as in a glass the glory of the Lord are changed into the same image from glory to glory, even as by the Spirit of the Lord" (2 Corinthians 3:18).

Second, we learn from these passages that increase in the love of God and in the love of our *neighbor* must go on together. One cannot increase in his love to God while there is a decrease in his love to his neighbor, nor increase in his love to his neighbor while his love to God is decreasing.

"By this we know that we love the children of God, when we love God and keep his commandments."

What a power the believers in Christ will be in this world, where such multitudes are hateful and hating one another, when they all come to abound in deep, pure, fervent love to God and to their neighbors! How they will be stimulated to labor and give and pray for the gathering of every creature in the world into the fold of Christ, when they love God the Father, the Son, and the Holy Spirit, "with all their heart, and soul, and might, and mind, and strength," and really and truly love their neighbor as themselves! An increase of such love will be accompanied by a vast increase of missionary zeal and enterprise; and not long would it be before there will be,

"Great voices in heaven, saying, The kingdoms of this world have become the kingdoms of our Lord and of his Christ; and he shall reign for ever and ever" (Revelation 11:15).

— CHAPTER

7

The Bible

We are all aware that no book on earth is clothed with such claims as the Bible, and none deals with subjects of such deep interest. Hence, it is man's plain duty to inform himself as to its authenticity and mission. It will be seen from the preceding chapters of this work how constantly the truths that it sets forth are drawn from the Bible. Therefore these pages are inserted here to aid the inquirer in his study of the facts of the Bible and in his earnest search for the blessed truths that God has here revealed to man.

(1) The Bible is a gracious revelation from God

This proposition is established by the following facts, namely:

(a) Man is made for a moral law—for a law which looks upon, judges, and rewards the thoughts and motives of the heart. He is made for a law that is higher in its authority, and more searching in its nature than the law of human governments. Of all the creatures on earth, man is especially the creature of conscience, perceiving the difference between right and wrong. This fact is evidence that there are desires and purposes and actions that are morally wrong, and other moral desires, purposes, and actions that are morally right; and the reproof and pain which we feel when we do wrong is evidence that it is required of us that we shall do right.

(b) As God is our Creator, it follows that his character is the standard of right and wrong. It is not necessary to use many words to sustain this statement, for all can readily see that there can be none above the Creator in anything, and especially none above him in matters of government. His character must give form and spirit to governments—out of his holy nature must flow the laws of his wide universe.

(c) A finite man is not able to search the heart of another man; how much less is a finite man able to know all the mind of the Infinite Jehovah? Hence, it follows that God must reveal himself to his creatures, or remain forever unknown to them.

"Canst thou by searching find out God? canst thou find out the Almighty unto perfection? It is as high as heaven; what canst thou do? Deeper than hell; what canst thou know?" (Job 11:7-9).

How can poor, feeble, finite, sinful, mortal man measure and understand the Infinite, the Mighty, the Eternal God? "Maybe," some one will say, "it is probable that God is hiding his character from his intelligent creatures." It is out of place for a man who stands in full view of the light of day to say that probably the sun has not risen. But allow the statement that God probably desires to hide his will from man touching man's moral conduct, and we shall see that we have set him against himself—God against God, the divine government against the divine government. How can he enforce his law against one to whom he has not revealed the law? I speak of intelligent beings.

(2) THE BIBLE CONTAINS MARKS OF THE DIVINE MIND:

(a) In the simplicity of its records.

The careful, thoughtful Bible student must be struck with the idea that every writer of the sacred book seems to feel himself perfectly free from any necessity of taking up the burden of proof regarding the truthfulness of his record. He simply makes his statements one after another, and seems not to have the least anxiety as to whether some one may not believe what he has written. The disciples who write of the Crucifixion take no pains to compare their books, so as to remove seeming contradictions, and hence one writes that one of the thieves reviled Jesus, while another writes that both the thieves reviled him. Every man seems to feel that it is not his to set up arguments. The reason for this is found only in what they themselves tell us about it; namely, that the book and the facts and the entire business *was* God's, not theirs.

(b) In the unity of its books.

Between the writing of the first and the last books of the Bible, more than fifteen hundred years elapsed, and it engaged the pens of shepherds, farmers, doctors, lawyers, priests, prophets, apostles, poor men, rich men, unlearned men, learned men, great men. Sometimes it is precept; sometimes it is history; sometimes it is biography; sometimes it is song; sometimes it is supplication, and sometimes it is prophecy: from Genesis to the Revelation, holiness is the moral seal, while everywhere grace, mercy, and hope shine in the face of the one Messiah.

(c) In its prophecy.

Man does not know the things of the future. The uncovering of future events is in the power of God alone. Compare the following concerning the bondage and the deliverance of the children of Israel:

"And when the sun was going down, a deep sleep fell upon Abram; and, lo, a horror of great darkness fell upon him. And he said unto Abram, Know of a surety that thy seed shall be a stranger in a land that is not theirs, and shall serve them; and they shall afflict them four hundred years; and also that nation, whom they shall serve, will I judge: and afterward shall they come out with great substance. And thou shalt go to thy fathers in peace; thou shalt be buried in a good old age. But in the fourth generation they shall come hither again: for the iniquity of the Amorites is not yet full. And it came to pass, that, when the sun went down, and it was dark, behold a smoking furnace, and a burning lamp that passed between those pieces" (Genesis 15:12-17).

"And the children of Israel were fruitful, and increased abundantly, and multiplied, and waxed exceeding mighty; and the land was filled with them. Now there arose up a new king over Egypt, which knew not Joseph. And he said unto his people, Behold, the people of the children of Israel are more and mightier than we; come on, let us deal wisely with them; lest they multiply, and it come to pass, that, when there falleth out any war, they join also unto our enemies, and fight against us, and so get them up out of the land. Therefore they did set over them taskmasters to afflict them with their burdens. And they built for Pharaoh treasure cities, Pithom and Raamses. But the more they afflicted them, the more they multiplied and grew. And they were grieved because of the children of Israel. And the Egyptians made the children of Israel to serve with rigour: and they made their lives bitter with hard bondage, in mortar, and in brick, and in all manner of service in the field: all their service, wherein they made them serve, was with rigour" (Exodus 1:7-14).

"Now the sojourning of the children of Israel, who dwelt in Egypt, *was* four hundred and thirty years. And it came to pass at the end of the four hundred and thirty years, even the selfsame day it came to pass, that all the hosts of the Lord went out from the land of Egypt. It *is* a night to be much observed unto the Lord for bringing them out from the land of Egypt: this *is* that night of the Lord to be observed of all the children of Israel in their generations" (Exodus 12:40–42).

These events extend over more than four hundred years of time. The prophecy was uttered about two hundred years before the bondage, and more than four hundred years before the redemption.

The following is more conspicuous in detail than that just referred to. It pertains to the capture of Babylon by Cyrus and the return of the Jews to Jerusalem. The prophecy is addressed to Israel, and begins:

"Thus saith the Lord, thy Redeemer, and he that formed thee from the womb, I am the Lord that maketh all *things*; that stretcheth forth the heavens alone; that spreadeth abroad the earth by myself; that saith to the deep, Be dry, and I will dry up thy rivers; that saith of Cyrus, *He is* my shepherd, and shall perform all my pleasure: even saying to Jerusalem, Thou shalt be built; and to the temple, Thy foundation shall be laid" (Isaiah 44:24, 27, 28).

"Thus saith the Lord to his anointed, to Cyrus, whose right hand I have holden, to subdue nations before him: and I will loose the loins of kings, to open before him the two-leaved gates; and the gates shall not be shut; I will go before thee, and make the crooked places straight: I will break in pieces the gates of brass, and cut in sunder the bars of iron: and I will give thee the treasures of darkness, and hidden riches of secret places, that thou mayest know that I, the Lord, which call *thee* by thy name, am the God of Israel. For Jacob my servant's sake, and Israel mine elect, I have even called thee by thy name: I have surnamed thee, though thou hast not known me. I *am* the Lord, and *there is* none else, *there is* no God besides me: I girded thee, though thou hast not known me; that they may know from the rising of the sun, and from the west, that *there is* none besides me. I am the Lord, and *there is* none else" (Isaiah 45:1–6).

"Now in the first year of Cyrus king of Persia, that the word of the Lord *spoken* by the mouth of Jeremiah might be accomplished, the Lord stirred up the spirit of Cyrus king of Persia, that he made a proclamation throughout all his kingdom, and *put it* also in writing, saying, Thus saith Cyrus king of

Persia, All the kingdoms of the earth hath the Lord God of heaven given me; and he hath charged me to build him a house in Jerusalem, which is in Judah. Who is there among you of all his people? The Lord his God be with him, and let him go up" (2 Chronicles 36:22, 23; see also Ezra 1:1-4).

The notable details referred to are these: Babylon was built on either side of the river Euphrates, and around it was a great wall. The part of the river which ran through the city had on either bank strong walls extending from one outer wall to the other. Streets led from one side of the city to the other, and crossed these river walls through heavy brazen gates. God mentions the river and the gates to Isaiah, telling that he will dry up the one and open the other before Cyrus. This is declared more than a hundred years before Cyrus is born, and about one hundred and fifty years before the taking of the city of Babylon by the Medes and Persians.

Profane historians tell us that the river was dried up, or turned from its bed; that the great brazen gates leading up from the river gave entrance to the Medo-Persian hosts under Darius and Cyrus. On the loosing of the loins of kings spoken of in these passages, see Daniel 5:6. The daylight does not more plainly and conclusively tell of the presence of the sun than this tells of the presence of the all-wise God.[1]

Where is Babylon? Where is Tyre? Where is the glory of Jerusalem? Where is the country of the Jews? Where are the princes of Egypt? Babylon is the habitation of bats, owls, and serpents. Tyre is as "the top of the rock, a place to spread nets upon." Jerusalem is a desolation. The temple is gone; "not one stone is left upon another that is not thrown down." Homeless and without a country, the Jew wanders in every land. For nearly three thousand years Egypt has bowed her neck under the yoke of foreign rulers.

(3) ON THE FULFILLMENT OF MESSIANIC PROPHECY

Christ appeared in a time that was made ready for him. The dispensation of types and shadows had finished its mission. Its rites and ceremonies were ordained to excite inquiry. They had done this. The Jews had found that they

---

1. If the reader has time and desire to pursue further the subject of prophecy, I refer him to Isaiah 13:19-22; Ezekiel 26:3-14; Zechariah 9:3, 4; Ezekiel 30:13. Compare these prophecies with what is known to-day with reference to the cities and peoples herein referred to. Compare Jerusalem and the present state of the Jews with Leviticus 26; Deuteronomy 28; Amos 9:9; and Luke 13:34, 35.

were only mysterious symbols, which, though they were indices, were possessed of no life-giving energy. Hence, in their consciousness of spiritual want, they had divided into many factions. There were the Pharisees, with their traditions and self-righteousness; the Sadducees, with their denial of a hereafter and of the existence of angels and spirits; the Galileans, with their exclusiveness, separation, and proscription; the Herodians, with their deception and duplicity, claiming the God of the Jews and practicing the morals of heathen; the scribes, with their pride and vanity in their lifeless learning; the Sanhedrin, or "Council," with their spirit of lording it over God's heritage; the publicans, with their extortion and oppression; the Samaritans, keeping up the old feud of the times of Jeroboam; and the Essenes, with their fanaticism and asceticism. The heathen intellectual sky was full of stars, such as Julius Caesar, Cicero, Virgil, Horace, Strabo, and others. "Many were running to and fro, and knowledge was increased." "The time was fulfilled." The times and wonders of Daniel's prophecy were at hand (Daniel 2, 7, 9, 12). The sceptre was on the eve of departing forever from Judah (Genesis 49:10).

This was not an age of credulity. It was a time rich and golden with thought. Had Christ been only a man, it were but the rising of a lone star in a lighted sky; but as he was the "Sun of Righteousness" it was as the orb of day ascending the eastern horizon, as the stars disappear in the excellent brightness of the day. Josephus, who lived about this time, says:

"Now there was about this time Jesus, a wise man, if it be lawful to call him a man, for he was a doer of wonderful works, a teacher of such men as receive the truth with pleasure. He drew over to him both many of the Jews and many of the Gentiles. He was (the) Christ. And when Pilate, at the suggestion of the principal men among us, had condemned him to the cross, those that loved him at the first did not forsake him, for he appeared to them alive again the third day, as the divine prophets had foretold these and ten thousand other wonderful things concerning him. And the tribe of Christians, so named from him, are not extinct at this day" ("Flavius Josephus," Book XVIII, Chap. 3, Sec. 3).

Now thus wrote Josephus, during the first century. He did not write with reference to Christianity. In a large book written by him, the above short notice is all the attention his pen gives to Christ or to Christians. He is a disinterested, but honest witness. He tells that which he and everybody else had accepted as true—namely, that the Christ who had been foretold by the "divine prophets" had really appeared in the person of Jesus of Nazareth; that, according to prophecy, he had been put to death on the cross, had been buried, had risen again, and had showed himself to the Christians, who still clung to him. He really tells substantially the very same story told by the disciples in the four gospels (1 Corinthians 15:3-5). About the same time that Josephus, the Jewish historian, wrote of the death and resurrection of Jesus, Tacitus, an illustrious Roman statesman and historian, also wrote that Christ was crucified in Judea by Pontius Pilate, during the reign of Tiberius. He speaks at length of the spread of Christianity in the Roman Empire, of the increasing number of Christians, and of the steadfastness of their faith; but could say nothing against their morals, against their loyalty, nor of the lack of authentic evidence as to the veracity of their Leader, or the truth of their doctrines (See "Annals" of Tacitus). Pliny and others wrote of them, but could bring no accusation against their morals, nor against the authenticity of their claims, touching the Jesus to whom Josephus refers. Why is it that neither Jew nor heathen can dispute Josephus' statement concerning Jesus and his resurrection? Again: The Christian inscriptions, Biblical scenes, and gospel relics, in the catacombs of Rome and Alexandria, are silent, but authentic witnesses for Christ, for Christianity, for the New Testament, and for the hope that lies beyond these mortal shores. I need not mention the fact that in two or three hundred years this doctrine of the resurrection of Jesus really overcame the great Roman Empire, capturing its king, making the fierce Roman eagle fold its wings, and droop at the foot of the cross. I need not mention that the cross came to these conquests without sword, without spear, without warwhoops, or any such things. I need not mention that they who loved Jesus overcame simply by the blood of the Lamb. Does human experience witness that falsehood conquers in this way, and that its victories make men purer and better? What other name and doctrines have conquered so gloriously in such a spirit, and by aid of such means?

Moreover, the millions of the various tongues and nations who at the present day believe in Jesus Christ, witness to the truthfulness of the New Testament records and New Testament doctrines. As the Jews marveled at Jesus' preaching, because of the fact that he was unlearned, he replied:

"My doctrine is not mine, but his that sent me. If any man will do his will, he shall know *of the doctrine whether it be of God or whether I speak of myself"* (John 7:16, 17).

"Handle me and see" (Luke 24:39).

This runs on the principle that the eating of an article is the only *sure proof* of its dietetic and nutritious claims. If a starving man should survive, strengthen, and fatten by the eating of oak leaves, the nutritious qualities of the leaves would be proven. Behold the millions of many ages who have fed upon Christ! One has only to stand before the ten commandments with a humble mind, and let these speak to his heart, and he must see that his soul is dead in trespasses and in sin. He must see that notwithstanding it is his plain duty to love God with all his heart, with all his mind, with all his soul, and with all his strength, and to love his fellow-man as he loves himself, yet he neither does nor can do either of these duties. He must see also that while he is neglecting his duty, and separated from God, he is separated from his true life, his peace, his happiness, and his prosperity. Millions of intelligent, conscientious men of all times and lands, and tongues and peoples, perceiving their helpless ruin and hearing that Jesus is the way, and the truth, and the life, have received him by faith, and in consequence are living witnesses that the doctrine is of God and is all that it claims to be. Before any man can dispute the claims of Christ and Christians, he must prove that the men and women who have given the world its richest blessings are all *fools, fanatics,* or *liars;* for the world owes more to Christianity than to all other creeds, and more to Christians than to all other sects among men. In the foundation of Scotland's greatness appear the personality, words, and life of John Knox. In the basis of the mighty German manhood lies the wonderful Martin Luther and the scholarly Melancthon. And England is the greatest nation of the Old World only because of the learning, diligence, heroism, and martyr spirit of her Wycliffe, her Tyndale, her Coverdale, her Cranmer, her Bunyan, and her other Christian men and women. And all these sprang into life and power only as they were touched by the Christ of the New Testament. Not a cloud, but *clouds* of saintly witnesses declare that Jesus Christ is the bread which came down from heaven, and that to all who receive him (even to them who believe on his name), he gives the power to become the sons of God (John 1:12, 13).

Nothing can be plainer than that this salvation is one that meets the crying needs of the human soul. We are not naturally the sons of God, and therefore how to become the possessors of this high privilege is the all-absorbing question of the heart and mind of man. The old question of the days of Job, "How shall man be just with God?" is answered only in the New Testament:

"By him all that believe are justified from all things from which *ye* could not be justified by the law of Moses" (Acts 13:39).

I repeat the statement that every person whose being and character are ennobled by the faith of Jesus Christ is a witness to the authenticity of the New Testament. The doctor can produce no evidences of skill, and leave no praises for his medicines so conclusive, as the health and strength of persons recovered from the power of dangerous diseases.

And this wonderful operation of turning sons of sin into sons of righteousness ought to end all controversy as to whether or not Jesus is the Messiah of the Old Testament.

(4) How the Law of God was given

(a) By the finger of God witnessed by his voice from Sinai's smoking top.

"And God spake all these words, saying,

"I *am* the Lord thy God, which have brought thee out of the land of Egypt, out of the house of bondage.

"Thou shalt have no other gods before me.

"Thou shalt not make unto thee any graven image, or any likeness *of any thing* that is in heaven above, or that *is* in the earth beneath, or that *is* in the water under the earth:

"Thou shalt not bow down thyself to them, nor serve them: for I the Lord thy God am a jealous God, visiting the iniquity of the fathers upon the children unto the third and fourth *generation* of them that hate me; and shewing mercy unto thousands of them that love me, and keep my commandments.

"Thou shalt not take the name of the Lord thy God in vain: for the Lord will not hold him guiltless that taketh his name in vain.

"Remember the sabbath day, to keep it holy. Six days shalt thou labour, and do all thy work: but the seventh day is the sabbath of the Lord thy God: in *it* thou shalt not do any work, thou, nor thy son, nor thy daughter, thy manservant, nor thy maidservant, nor thy cattle, nor thy stranger that *is* within thy gates: for in six days the Lord made heaven and earth, the sea, and all that in them *is,* and rested the seventh day: wherefore the Lord blessed the sabbath day, and hallowed it.

"Honour thy father and thy mother: that thy days may be long upon the land which the Lord thy God giveth thee.

"Thou shalt not kill.

"Thou shalt not commit adultery.

"Thou shalt not steal.

"Thou shalt not bear false witness against thy neighbour.

"Thou shalt not covet thy neighbour's house, thou shalt not covet thy neighbor's wife, nor his manservant, nor his maidservant, nor his ox, nor his ass, nor any thing that is thy neighbour's.

"And all the people saw the thunderings, and the lightnings, and the noise of the trumpet, and the mountain smoking: and when the people saw it, they removed, and stood afar off. And they said unto Moses, Speak thou with us and we will hear: but let not God speak with us, lest we die" (Exodus 20:1–19).

"And he gave unto Moses, when he had made an end of communing with him upon mount Sinai, two tables of testimony, tables of stone, written with the finger of God" (Exodus 31:18).

(b) By the inspiration of God vouchsafed to holy men.

"Now these be the last words of David. David the son of Jesse said, and the man who was raised up on high, the anointed of the God of Jacob, and the sweet psalmist of Israel, said, The Spirit of the Lord spake by me, and his word was in my tongue" (2 Samuel 23:1, 2).

"Then the spirit took me up, and I heard behind me a voice of a great rushing, saying, Blessed be the glory of the Lord from his place. I heard also the noise of the wings of the living creatures that touched one another, and the noise of the wheels over against them, and a noise of a great rushing. So the spirit lifted me up, and took me away, and I went in bitterness, in the heat of my spirit; but the hand of the Lord was strong upon me.

"Then I came to them of the captivity at Tel-abib, that dwelt by the river of Chebar, and I sat where they sat, and remained there astonished among them seven days. And it came to pass at the end of seven days, that the word of the Lord came unto me, saying, Son of man, I have made thee a watchman unto the house of Israel: therefore hear the word at my mouth, and give them warning from me. When I say unto the wicked, Thou shalt surely die; and thou giveth him not warning, nor speakest to warn the wicked from his wicked way, to save his life; the same wicked man shall die in his iniquity; but his blood will I require at thine hand. Yet if thou warn the wicked, and he turn not from his wickedness, nor from his wicked way, he shall die in his iniquity; but thou hast delivered thy soul. Again, when a righteous man doth turn from his righteousness, and commit iniquity, and I lay a stumblingblock before him, he shall die: because thou hast not given him warning, he shall die in his sin, and his righteousness which he hath done shall not be remembered; but his blood will I require at thine hand. Nevertheless, if thou warn the righteous *man,* that the righteous sin not, and he doth not sin, he shall surely live, because he is warned; also thou hast delivered thy soul" (Ezekiel 3:12–21).

"We have also a more sure word of prophecy; whereunto ye do well that ye take heed, as unto a light that shineth in a dark place, until the day dawn, and the daystar arise in your hearts: Knowing this first, that no prophecy of the Scripture is of any private interpretation. For the prophecy came not in old time by the will of man: but holy men of God spake *as they were* moved by the Holy Ghost" (2 Peter 1:19–21).

Here we are plainly taught that God communicated his thoughts, his mind, to holy men, who wrote and spoke as his mind dictated in them and as the Holy Spirit moved and superintended them. This word is as perfect *as* that which his finger wrote in stone or his voice uttered on the mount. In both cases it is God overruling his creatures—the human mind now, the winds then.

(c) Given by the Son of God.

"God, who at sundry times and in divers manners spake in time past unto the fathers by the prophets, hath in these last days spoken unto us by *his* Son, whom he hath appointed heir of all things, by whom also he made the worlds; who being the brightness of *his* glory, and the express image of his person, and upholding all things by the word of his power, when he had by himself purged our sins, sat down on the right hand of the Majesty on high" (Hebrews 1:1–3).

May God duly impress our minds and affections with the majesty of the manner of the giving of the sacred word Jehovah writes with his own finger, speaks to the assembled hosts in his own voice, then breathes his thoughts into the minds of his servants, the prophets—elevating, superintending, and guiding them; and, last of all, he sends into the world his only-begotten and well-beloved Son, the Word, who was in the beginning with God and was God, and speaks to us by him, giving us the last things!

"Therefore we ought to give the more earnest heed to the things which we have heard, lest at any time we should let *them* slip. For if the word spoken by angels was steadfast, and every transgression and disobedience received a just recompense of reward; how shall we escape, if we neglect so great salvation; which at the first began to be spoken by the Lord, and was confirmed unto us by them that heard *him*; God also bearing *them* witness, both with signs and wonders and with divers miracles, and gifts of the Holy Ghost, according to his own will?" (Hebrews 2:1–4).

We need not expect any further revelations. The book of truth has gone on unfolding the counsels of God to human view, till we have come into the midst of the beauties and glories of redemption. Thenceforward, even unto the end, the disciples, under the guidance of the Holy Spirit, are to be busied in the work of interpreting the Scriptures that God has given us, and in earnest efforts to make the truths which are therein taught, known throughout all the world.

(5) For what purpose the Bible was given

It was designed to be a complete treasury of heavenly instruction, our only and all-sufficient rule of faith and practice.

(a) It teaches us of God.

Our chapter on the "Being and Character of God" was made up from the teachings of his sacred book. Take away the Bible, and we do not know, and cannot know all those things that are so important for us to learn concerning our Maker and Saviour and Judge. In this book it is made distinctly known to us that there are not gods many and lords many, as the nations without the Bible have supposed, but that the Lord our God is one God, and he is revealed to us in three glorious persons—the Father, the Son, and the Holy Spirit. From the Bible's sacred pages we learn that our God is holy and just, true and faithful, good and gracious, unchangeable and full of love, that he himself is Love.

(b) Of his personal or particular providence.

There are some who teach that the Sovereign Lord of heaven and earth pays no attention to this world that he has created, or to the affairs of the men whom he has formed and fashioned and placed in the world. They say that he made the world and all that therein is, that he put in it certain laws that were conducive to animal and vegetable increase, and then turned away and left it to the operation of those laws, or to chance, or to "the survival of the fittest." But this book gives us a far different view of the care of God for the world that he has formed. It tells us of his continual watchcare and oversight. So far from withdrawing from the world, God is constantly present and exercising minute care.

"O Lord, thou hast searched me, and known *me*. Thou knowest my downsitting and mine uprising, thou understandest my thoughts afar off. Thou compassest my path and my lying down, and art acquainted *with* all my ways. For *there is* not a word in my tongue, *but*, lo, O Lord, thou knowest it altogether. Thou hast beset me behind and before, and laid thine hand upon me. *Such* knowledge *is* too wonderful for me; it is high, I cannot *attain* unto it. Whither shall I go from thy spirit? or whither shall I flee from thy presence? If I ascend up into heaven, thou *art* there: if I make my bed in hell, behold thou *art there*. *If* I take the wings of the morning, *and* dwell in the uttermost parts of the sea; even there shall thy hand lead me, and thy right hand shall hold me. If I say, Surely the darkness shall cover me; even the night shall be light about me. Yea, the darkness hideth not from thee; but the night shineth as the day: the darkness and the light *are* both alike *to thee*" (Psalm 139:1–12).

This passage gives a nobler view of the character of God; for it indicates that he feels and manifests a deep and abiding, a true fatherly interest in those to whom he has given life and all the wonderful powers of life.

The statement that is made in regard to the mission of the well-beloved Son of God, to his work while he dwelt on earth, and to the position and authority that are his since his return to the presence of the Father, bears clear testimony to the close connection that God maintains with the world and the dwellers in it. Jesus Christ is "made head over all things to the church." He watches over every member of that church, and orders everything so as to make "all things work together for good to them that love God, to them who are the called according to his purpose" (Romans 8:28). Jesus tells them: "The very hairs of your head are all numbered" (Matthew 10:30). The Psalmist says: "Like as a father pitieth his children, so the Lord pitieth them that fear him" (Psalm 103:13).

The existence of the Bible, and the scheme of redemption that it reveals, give to every unprejudiced mind conclusive proof that God, when he had created and peopled the world, did not turn away and leave it to be governed by mere natural laws, by chance, or by "the survival of the fittest," but that he exercises over it a minute, constant, and loving care. The Bible teaches us this, and the truth should be clearly recognized by men, and be ever gratefully acknowledged by them.

(c) Of the duties and relations of life.

The Psalmist had a very great love for the word of God that had been made known unto him. He spoke of its great value to him in words that have often been quoted, and should be accepted as true by every one who is traveling through this world where so much is dark.

"Thy word is a lamp unto my feet, and a light unto my path" (Psalm 119:105).

The terms in which he speaks of it shows how he loved the "word," or "law," or "commandments," or "statutes" of God. He desired to walk safely through the world, and did not think he could avoid stumbling without the light which the word of God shed on his path.

"Wherewith shall a young man cleanse his way? by taking heed thereto according to thy word. ... Thy word have I hid in mine heart, that I might not sin against thee. ... O how love I thy law! it is my meditation all the day. Thou through thy commandments hast made me wiser than mine enemies: for they are ever with me. I have more understanding than all my teachers: for thy testimonies are my meditation. I understand more than the ancients, because I keep thy precepts. I have refrained my feet from every evil way, that I might keep thy word. I have not departed from thy judgments: for thou hast taught me. How sweet are thy words unto my taste! yea, sweeter than honey to my mouth! Through thy precepts I get understanding: therefore I hate every false way. ... Thy testimonies are wonderful: therefore doth my soul keep them. The entrance of thy words giveth light; it giveth understanding unto the simple. I opened my mouth, and panted: for I longed for thy commandments. ... Order my steps in thy word: and let not any iniquity have dominion over me" (Psalm 119:9, 11; 97–104, 129–131, 133).

The Apostle Paul exhorts believers in Ephesus to take to themselves the whole armor of God, among whose parts is "the sword of the Spirit, which is the word of God" (Ephesians 6:17). The word is a sword for the contest with temptation and sin; the leaven of harmony for bringing about the unity of the saints; and the supreme standard of righteousness by which to try human creeds, conduct, and opinions. It teaches the ruler how to rule, and the subject how to obey. It teaches the husband how to treat his wife, and the wife how she is to comport herself toward her husband. It teaches the parent how to act toward his child, and the child how to honor his parent. It has a lesson for the rich and for the poor; for the high and for the low; for the sick and for those in health; for the sinner and for the saint; for the joyous and for those in deep sorrow; for the master and for the slave; for the host and for the stranger; for the wise and for the unwise; for the weak and for the strong—a lesson for all.

There is none in a condition so high that he does not need the lessons which the Bible teaches for his instruction as to his duties toward men and toward God. After Joshua had come to Moses's stead it is said:

"Now after the death of Moses the servant of the Lord, it came to pass, that the Lord spake unto Joshua the son of Nun, Moses' minister, saying, Moses my servant is dead; now therefore arise, go over this Jordan, thou, and all this people, unto the land which I do give to them, *even* to the children of Israel. Every place that the sole of your foot shall tread upon, that have I given unto you as I said unto Moses. ... Only be thou strong and very courageous, that thou mayest observe to do according to all the law, which Moses my servant commanded thee: turn not from it *to* the right hand, or *to* the left, that thou mayest prosper whithersoever thou goest. This book of the law shall not depart out of thy mouth; but thou shalt meditate therein day and night, that thou mayest observe to do according to all that is written therein: for then thou shalt make thy way prosperous, and then thou shalt have good success. Have not I commanded thee? Be strong and of a good courage; be not afraid, neither be thou dismayed: for the Lord thy God *is* with thee whithersoever thou goest" (Joshua 1:1–3, 7–9).

Just before Paul was taken away, he wrote to Timothy to impress on him an important lesson:

"But continue thou in the things which thou hast learned and hast been assured of, knowing of whom thou hast learned *them*; and that from a child thou hast known the holy Scriptures, which are able to make thee wise unto salvation through faith which is in Christ Jesus. All Scripture *is* given by inspiration of God, and *is* profitable for doctrine, for reproof, for correction, for instruction in righteousness: that the man of God may be perfect, thoroughly furnished unto all good works" (2 Timothy 3:14–17).

This brave soldier of the cross, who was now about to pass into the presence of his Lord, looked back and assured his younger brother that he was willing to leave him to the saving, quickening, sanctifying power of the Holy Scriptures.

To come down to our own times, we may mention the case of a poor unlearned working man, who had been for many years walking through life with no regard to that lamp and light which the Psalmist so highly prized. A Christian friend who had been wont to speak to him of the salvation of God and to lend or give him Christian books once met him after a long absence. He asked whether he found time still to read, designing to put some good book in his hands. "No," said he, with earnestness and simplicity, "not much now. I never had been brought up to read the Bible, or to care how I lived. But I have learned that I ought to serve the Lord; and now when I want to know how he wants me to live, I find I have to be reading the Bible every day; and I do not get much time to read anything else." That sacred book had become to him a lamp to his feet and a light to his path. They and they only walk safely who walk by the light that God has given in his sacred word.

In closing the chapter on the Bible, in which we have sought to call attention to the fullness of its teachings, we submit the following closing words of the last book of the sacred volume, which may well be thought over carefully by any who are tempted to tamper with any portion of the Book of God.

"For I testify unto every man that heareth the words of the prophecy of this book. If any man shall add unto these things, God shall add unto him the plagues that are written in this book: and if any man shall take away from the words of the book of this prophecy, God shall take away his part out of the book of life, and out of the holy city, and *from* the things which are written in this book. He which testifieth these things saith, Surely I come quickly: Amen. Even so, come, Lord Jesus. The grace of our Lord Jesus Christ *be* with you all. Amen" (Revelation 22:18–21).

8

The Christian Church

(1) THE MEANING OF THE WORD CHURCH

(a) The word is sometimes used to include the whole family of the redeemed of all ages. Let us notice some examples:

"He saith unto them, But whom say ye that I am? And Simon Peter answered and said, Thou art the Christ, the Son of the living God. And Jesus answered and said unto him, Blessed art thou, Simon Bar-jona: for flesh and blood hath not revealed *it* unto thee, but my Father which is in heaven. And I say also unto thee, That thou art Peter, and upon this rock I will build my church; and the gates of hell shall not prevail against it. And I will give unto thee the keys of the kingdom of heaven: and whatsoever thou shalt bind on earth shall be bound in heaven: and whatsoever thou shalt loose on earth shall be loosed in heaven" (Matthew 16:15-19).

The church spoken of here is the whole family of the redeemed, who are to be builded upon that faith (called a rock) which Peter professed, and built together in it. The word "kingdom," in the verse 19, as quoted above, is but a repetition of the same idea. In this sense church means "kingdom of God" or "kingdom of heaven," meaning the kingdom of grace. In the following the word church has the same meaning:

"But ye are come unto mount Sion, and unto the city of the living God, the heavenly Jerusalem, and to an innumerable company of angels. To the general assembly and church of the firstborn, which are written in heaven, and to God the Judge of all, and to the spirits of just men made perfect, and to

Jesus the mediator of the new covenant, and to the blood of sprinkling, that speaketh better things than *that* of Abel" (Hebrews 12:22–24).

(b) The term is used for a body of believers, united together in one place according to the teachings of the New Testament.

"And if he shall neglect to hear them, tell *it* unto the church: but if he neglect to hear the church, let him be unto thee as a heathen man and a publican" (Matthew 18:17).

"And when they were come, and had gathered the church together, they rehearsed all that God had done with them, and how he had opened the door of faith unto the Gentiles" (Acts 14:27).

"John to the seven churches which are in Asia: Grace be unto you, and peace, from him which is, and which was, and which is to come; and from the seven Spirits which are before his throne" (Revelation 1:4).

By carefully reading the first three chapters of the Revelation, we shall see that what are called churches are local organizations or companies of Christian believers—not different denominations of believers. We shall see also that all that pertains to their government, including the selection of officers and discipline, were purely local. The Saviour called upon each body separately to correct its faith and morals, making no references whatever either to councils or conferences of churches or ministers.

(2) The members of a church of Christ

(a) Qualifications of members of a church.

Each church must receive its model from the kingdom of grace, of which it is a type. The kingdom of grace is composed of such as are meek, broken-hearted, repentant, and believing.

"Then Peter said unto them, Repent, and be baptized every one of you in the name of Jesus Christ for the remission of sins, and ye shall receive the gift of the Holy Ghost ... Then they that gladly received his word were baptized: and the same day there were added *unto them* about three thousand souls" (Acts 2:38, 41).

The members of a church of Christ must be such as really repent of their sins and gladly receive the word of the gospel, and are baptized in accordance with the command of Christ.

The following, by Dr. J. M. Frost, in "The Alabama Baptist," may be of use to some who desire to know precisely what baptism is:

"Archie Butler ('Sermons,' first series, page 88) says 'Now we are said to be "risen with Christ" out of our baptismal burial with him.'

"Canon Farrar ('Life and Letters of Paul,' page 480) renders Romans 6:4 as follows: 'The life of the Christian being hid with Christ in God, his death with Christ is a death to sin, his resurrection with Christ is a resurrection to life. The dipping under the waters of baptism is his union with Christ's death; his rising out of the waters of baptism is a resurrection with Christ, and the birth to a new life.'

"Archbishop Tillotson ('Bailey's Manual,' page 202) says: 'Anciently, those who were baptized were immersed in the water to represent their death to sin, and then did rise up out of the water to signify their entrance upon a new life; and to these customs the apostle alludes, Romans 6:4.'

"Conybeare and Howson ('Life and Epistles of Paul,' 384) says: 'Baptism was (unless in exceptional cases) administered by immersion, the convert being plunged beneath the surface of the water to represent his death to the life of sin, and then raised from the momentary burial to represent his resurrection to the life of righteousness.'

"Dean Stanley says: 'They plunged into a bath of purification, under the sanction of him into whom they were by that solemn rite baptized. ... The water in those Eastern regions, so doubly significant of all that was pure and refreshing, closed over the heads of the converts, and they rose into the light of heaven new and altered beings. Such was apostolic baptism. We are able, in detail, to track its history through the next three centuries.'

"Bishop Smith, of Kentucky, says: 'We have only to go back six or eight hundred years, and immersion was the only mode, except in cases of the few baptized on their beds, when death was near. And with regard to such cases, it disqualified its recipient for holy orders in case he recovered.' "

These extracts are all taken from authors belonging to the Church of England, except the last from a Bishop of the Protestant Episcopal Church in this country. With the view of the act of baptism here given the best lexicons and the ablest Greek scholars agree.

(3) THE OFFICERS OF A CHURCH

A consideration of the work to be done by the church may help us to see what officers are necessary. The church's appointed work, as is apparent in the

Great Commission, is to evangelize the world. This work of evangelization contains two distinct departments—namely, the work of proclaiming the gospel to sinners, and the work of edifying the saints. In both cases the main thing to be done is to proclaim and teach the gospel of Christ. This calls for teachers. This is the spiritual side.

But the saints who must be edified live in bodies of flesh which must be fed, clothed, housed, and cared for. In other words, because the church is wearing the form of matter, there is of necessity a material side as well as a spiritual side. This calls for men to serve tables, men to look after money, lands, houses of worship, and temporal affairs in general.

(a) The pastor.

This officer is to devote himself to labors for promoting the spiritual welfare of the church. We get a view of some of the leading features of his work from the following passages:

"But we will give ourselves continually to prayer, and to the ministry of the word" (Acts 6:4).

"Take heed therefore unto yourselves, and to all the flock, over the which the Holy Ghost hath made you overseers, to feed the church of God, which he hath purchased with his own blood" (Acts 20:28).

Here we see that they are to give themselves to communion with God in prayer, and to the teaching of the word. They are overseers of the flock of precious price, the flock which Christ has purchased with his own blood. And they are made overseers by the Holy Spirit. Thus we are taught how they must occupy themselves; they are to remember the value of the flock and to labor as under the eye of the Spirit, and take great heed. The following shows the purpose of their labor:

"And he gave some, apostles; and some, prophets; and some, evangelists; and some, pastors and teachers; for the perfecting of the saints, for the work of the ministry, for the edifying of the body of Christ: till we all come in the unity of the faith, and of the knowledge of the Son of God, unto a perfect man, unto the measure of the stature of the fulness of Christ: that we *henceforth* be no more children, tossed to and fro, and carried about with every wind of doctrine, by the sleight of men, *and* cunning craftiness, whereby they lie in wait to deceive; but speaking the truth in love, may grow up into him in all things, which is the head, *even* Christ: from whom the whole body fitly joined together and compacted by that which every joint supplieth, according to the effectual working in the measure of every part, maketh increase of the body unto the edifying of itself in love" (Ephesians 4:11–16).

They are to nourish and build up the flock into the unity of the faith, and the knowledge of the Son of God, seeking to raise the members "unto the measure of the stature of the fulness of Christ."

Their qualifications are given:

"This is a true saying, If a man desire the office of a bishop, he desireth a good work. A bishop then must be blameless, the husband of one wife, vigilant, sober, of good behaviour, given to hospitality, apt to teach; not given to wine, no striker, not greedy of filthy lucre; but patient, not a brawler, not covetous; one that ruleth well his own house, having his children in subjection with all gravity; (for if a man know not how to rule his own house, how shall he take care of the church of God?) Not a novice, lest being lifted up with pride he fall into the condemnation of the devil. Moreover he must have a good report of them which are without; lest he fall into reproach and the snare of the devil" (1 Timothy 3:1–7, 14, 15).

There are ten things the bishop must be, and six things he must not be. (1) He must be blameless, denying all ungodliness and worldly lust. (2) He must be the husband of one wife. (3) He must be a watchful, industrious, wide-awake man. (4) He must be a cool-headed, self-possessed man. (5) He must be a man of modest, manly behavior. (6) He must be a hospitable, liberal, kind-hearted man. (7) He must be fitted to the work of teaching. (8) He must be a patient man, a man who can hold to the right, reward or no reward, in joy or in sorrow. (9) He must be a good ruler, controlling his children. (10) He must have a good name without the church.

Then: (1) He must not be a slave to his appetites. (2) He must not be a mere apprentice in the truth, but must be a master; otherwise it will be the blind leading the blind. (3) He must not be a worshiper of money; for such a man will preach to *please* rather than preach to *profit*. (4) He must not be a mere brawler, but a teacher, rightly dividing the word of truth, to the edification of his hearers. (5) He must not be greedy of earthly gain. (6) He must not be a novice, unfitted to the gospel yoke and unused to the sufferings of the cross; for such an office will lead a man of unchastened spirit into unseemly pride, instead of the meekness and lowliness beseeming an humble minister of the word. He will be in danger of thinking more of himself than of Christ and the flock.

Let the minister heed the following from Paul, and imitate his example:

"For though I be free from all *men, yet* have I made myself servant unto all, that I might gain the more. To the weak became I as weak, that I might gain the weak: I am made all things to all *men,* that I might by all means save some. I therefore so run, not as uncertainly: so fight I, not as one that beateth the air: but I keep under my body, and bring *it* into subjection: lest that by any means, when I have preached to others, I myself should be a castaway" (1 Corinthians 9:19, 22, 26, 27).

"For the love of Christ constraineth us; because we thus judge, that if one died for all, then were all dead: and *that* he died for all, that they which live should not henceforth live unto themselves, but unto him that died for them and rose again" (2 Corinthians 5:14, 15).

(b) Deacons.

The origin of the deacon's office is given as follows:

"And in those days, when the number of the disciples was multiplied, there arose a murmuring of the Grecians against the Hebrews, because their widows were neglected in the daily ministration. Then the twelve called the multitude of the disciples *unto them,* and said, It is not reason that we should leave the word of God, and serve tables. Wherefore, brethren, look ye out among you seven men of honest report, full of the Holy Ghost and wisdom, whom we may appoint over this business" (Acts 6:1-3).

During the time referred to here, the disciples had all things common — that is to say, they all lived from a common fund. The number of believers had greatly increased. Jews from Grecian cities had come to Jerusalem, and joined themselves to the followers of Christ. The daily divisions of the common fund, as each one had need, grew to be a great business in itself. "The daily ministration," added to the constant teaching and healing, was too much labor for the apostles. Hence, there was imperfect service — some strangers being missed, followed by complainings from those who had been neglected. Out of this state of things came necessity for the deacon's office. They were chosen to look after the temporal affairs of the saints. The following shows the office still further on:

"Likewise *must* the deacons be grave, not double-tongued, not given to much wine, not greedy of filthy lucre; holding the mystery of the faith in a pure conscience. And let these also first be proved; then let them use the office of a deacon, being *found* blameless. ... Let the deacons be the husbands of one wife, ruling their children and their own houses well. For they that have used the office of a deacon well purchase to themselves a good degree, and great boldness in the faith which is in Christ Jesus" (1 Timothy 3:8–10, 12, 13).

This office has ten qualifications, seven positive, and three negative. The positive are as follows: (1) He must have a good report for honesty; for otherwise the members cannot trust him with their property; and beside this, there may have been some reason for the evil reports. (2) He must be wise—that is, he must know how to manage business and how to satisfy those who trust him with their property. (3) He needs to be full of the Holy Spirit, lest his constant dealing with temporal matters, and the negligence and complainings of the people, should cause him to grow cold, formal, and spiritless. (4) He must be grave—that is, weighty and gentle in speech. (5) He must be a conscientious man, doing his service as unto God and not to men. (6) He must be one who respects the divine law, having but one wife. (7) He must be one who seeks to train his children in all good things.

The negative qualities are pointed out. (1) He must not be double tongued, talking one way to one and another way to another. He must be a man whose "yes" is yes, and whose "no" is no. (2) He must not be a slave of strong drink. (3) He must not be a man who may be turned from his righteousness by the love of money.

There are some things in connection with the deacons to be considered. (1) The deacon is elected by the church, and may be dismissed by the same if the members desire, or if the good of the cause should require. (2) The deacon has no spiritual authority by virtue of his office. Further than the management of such temporal affairs as the church may put into their hands, they are only brethren. (3) It is the duty of the church to see to it that the deacon is duly instructed in the things of his office.

(4) THE WORK OF THE CHURCH

(a) The church is to maintain the public worship of God and the proper observance of the ordinances of the gospel.

"Let us draw near with a true heart in full assurance of faith, having our hearts sprinkled from an evil conscience, and our bodies washed with pure water. Let us hold fast the profession of *our* faith without wavering; for he *is* faithful that promised; and let us consider one another to provoke unto love and to good works: not forsaking the assembling of ourselves together, as the manner of some is; but exhorting *one another:* and so much the more, as ye see the day approaching" (Hebrews 10:22–25).

"Be ye followers of me, even as I also am of Christ. Now I praise you, brethren, that ye remember me in all things, and keep the ordinances, as I delivered *them* to you" (1 Corinthians 11:1, 2).

The church cannot—if she remains faithful to Christ—permit her members to disregard these plain precepts of her Lord. She must have the members attend faithfully the public services of the sanctuary, and duly observe the Lord's Supper. It is also incumbent on the church in the admission of members to see that the ordinance of baptism is properly administered, according to the command and example of Christ, the Great Head of the Church.

(b) To provide a house of worship and other necessary conveniences for the assembly, for the residence of the pastor, and for the administration of the ordinances.

The record of the wilderness contains one chapter which confers much honor upon the children of Israel. It is the chapter which tells of the building of the tabernacle.

"And Moses spake unto all the congregation of the children of Israel, saying, This is the thing which the Lord commanded, saying, Take ye from among you an offering unto the Lord: whosoever is of a willing heart, let him bring it, an offering of the Lord. ... And all the congregation of the children of Israel departed from the presence of Moses. And they came, every one whose heart stirred him up, and every one whom his spirit made willing, *and* they brought the Lord's offering to the work of the tabernacle of the congregation, and for all his service, and for the holy garments. And they came, both men and women, as many as were willing hearted, *and* brought bracelets, and earrings, and rings, and tablets, all jewels of gold: and every man that offered, *offered an* offering of gold unto the Lord. And every man, with whom *was* found blue, and purple, and scarlet, and fine linen, and goats' *hair*, and red skins of rams, and badgers' skins, brought *them*. Every one that did offer an offering of silver and brass brought the Lord's offering: and every man, with whom was found shittim wood for any work of the service, brought *it*. And all the women that were wise-hearted did spin with their hands, and brought that which they had spun, *both* of blue, and of purple, *and* of scarlet, and of fine linen" (Exodus 35:4, 5, 20-25).

"And they spake unto Moses, saying, The people bring much more than enough for the service of the work, which the Lord commanded to make. And Moses gave commandment, and they caused it to be proclaimed throughout the camp, saying, Let neither man nor woman make any more work for the offering of the sanctuary. So the people were restrained from bringing. For the stuff they had was sufficient for all the work to make it, and too much" (Exodus 36:5-7).

The comforts and conveniences of God's house may greatly assist the gracious influences of his word, and be helpful in the accomplishment of good spiritual results.

(c) The church should make some suitable provision for the poor and helpless of its members.

The Lord God has been careful in all ages to speak on behalf of the poor. His ear has ever been open unto their cries, and his eye has always watched over their trying lot; and no wonder, for they are here to serve a purpose of the Divine Mind. Doubtless, they are a means for the cultivation of emotions of pity, sympathy, and compassion, and for the development of benevolence and love.

The poor, the blind, the lame, appear among us to draw our souls out of the narrow, cold, dark, sickly, damp dungeons of selfishness into the clear sunlight of love and mercy. It is in benevolence and love that the spiritual deficiency of Christians is often sadly manifest. It is worthy of note that Christ represents the last judgment as bestowing its rewards and its punishments in proportion as men have abounded or been lacking in benevolence and love.

"Inasmuch as ye have done it unto one of the least of these my brethren, ye have done it unto me" (Matthew 25:40).

"He that hath mercy on the poor, happy is he" (Proverbs 14:21).

"Blessed is he that considereth the poor: the Lord will deliver him in time of trouble" (Psalm 41:1).

"Now concerning the collection for the saints, as I have given order to the churches of Galatia, even so do ye. Upon the first *day* of the week let every one of you lay by him in store, as *God* hath prospered him, that there be no gatherings when I come" (1 Corinthians 16:1, 2).

(d) To provide for the support of the pastor, that he may give himself wholly unto prayer and to the study and ministry of the word. The reader is referred to the following Scriptures:

"Who goeth a warfare any time at his own charges? who planteth a vineyard, and eateth not of the fruit thereof? or who feedeth a flock, and eateth not of the milk of the flock? Say I these things as a man? or saith not the law the same also? For it is written in the law of Moses, Thou shalt not muzzle the mouth of the ox that treadeth out the corn. Doth God take care for oxen? Or saith he it altogether for our sakes? For our sakes, no doubt, this is written: that he that plougheth should plough in hope; and that he that thresheth in hope should be partaker of his hope. If we have sown unto you spiritual things, is it a great thing if we shall reap your carnal things? Do ye not know that they which minister about holy things live *of the things* of the temple? and they which wait at the altar are partakers with the altar? Even so hath the Lord ordained that they which preach the gospel should live of the gospel" (1 Corinthians 9:7-14).

"Go your ways: behold, I send you forth as lambs among wolves. Carry neither purse, nor scrip, nor shoes: and salute no man by the way. And into whatsoever house ye enter, first say, Peace *be* to this house. And if the son of peace be there, your peace shall rest upon it: if not, it shall turn to you again. And in the same house remain, eating and drinking such things as they give: for the labourer is worthy of his hire. Go not from house to house" (Luke 10:3-7).

"Heal the sick, cleanse the lepers, raise the dead, cast out devils: freely ye have received, freely give. Provide neither gold, nor silver, nor brass, in your purses; nor scrip for *your* journey, neither two coats, neither shoes, nor yet staves: for the workman is worthy of his meat" (Matthew 10:8-10).

"Let the elders that rule well be counted worthy of double honour, especially they who labour in the word and doctrine. For the Scripture saith, Thou shalt not muzzle the ox that treadeth out the corn. And, The labourer *is* worthy of his reward" (1 Timothy 5:17, 18).

"Let him that is taught in the word communicate unto him that teacheth in all good things. Be not deceived; God is not mocked: for whatsoever a man soweth, that shall he also reap. For he that soweth to his flesh shall of the flesh reap corruption; but he that soweth to the Spirit shall of the Spirit reap life everlasting" (Galatians 6:6-8).

The lessons taught herein are too plain to be misunderstood by any. Jesus charged the disciples to carry nothing with them for their daily needs, for the reason that their services entitled them to a proper support. And he who was taught in the word was to communicate to his teacher in all good (needful) things.

Common sense teaches us that if the pastor be constantly bound to the earth in toiling for bread, he cannot give that time to pastoral work and to the study of the Scriptures which is necessary to the greatest and surest spiritual success.

Under the Old Dispensation the whole tribe of Levi was set apart to the work of the temple, and the other eleven tribes had to minister to their needs (Numbers 35). Their support was provided for by a tax of one-tenth of all the increase of the land.

"And all the tithe of the land, *whether* of the seed of the land, or of the fruit of the tree, is the Lord's: it is holy unto the Lord. And concerning the tithe of the herd, or of the flock, *even* of whatsoever passeth under the rod, the tenth shall be holy unto the Lord" (Leviticus 27:30, 32).

"And the Lord spake unto Aaron, Behold, I also have given thee the charge of mine heave offerings of all the hallowed things of the children of Israel; unto thee have I given them by reason of the anointing, and to thy sons, by an ordinance for ever. ... And the Lord spake unto Aaron, Thou shalt have no inheritance in their land, neither shalt thou have any part among them: I am thy part and thine inheritance among the children of Israel. And, behold, I have given the children of Levi all the tenth in Israel for an inheritance, for their service which they serve, *even* the service of the tabernacle of the congregation" (Numbers 18:8, 20, 21).

When the teachings of the Scriptures in regard to the priests of the Mosaic Dispensation and the pastors of the churches of Christ come to be clearly understood, those churches that really take the Bible for their guide will cheerfully adopt measures for the support of their pastors. In the great day of account the Lord, who recognizes the giving of a cup of cold water to a disciple as a gift conferred on himself, will assuredly regard the funds for the support of the pastors that he in his grace gives to his churches as offerings made to himself, and will reward them accordingly.

(e) To provide for the religious education of the young.

Judging from the words of the angel unto Zacharias concerning John the Baptist, we may see that one of the great blessings to come to men out of the gospel is that the hearts of the fathers are to be turned toward their children.

"And he shall go before him in the spirit and power of Elias, to turn the hearts of the fathers to the children, and the disobedient to the wisdom of the just; to make ready a people prepared for the Lord" (Luke 1:17).

If the word of God is put into the youthful heart, its effects will be manifest in all the springs and fountains and energies and powers of the mind and affections. God has ever been careful for the training of the youth, and the churches of the Lord should all give this work their earnest support.

"Therefore shall ye lay up these my words in your heart and in your soul, and bind them for a sign upon your hand, that they may be as frontlets between your eyes. And ye shall teach them your children, speaking of them when thou sittest in thine house, and when thou walkest by the way, when thou liest down, and when thou risest up. And thou shalt write them upon the door posts of thine house, and upon thy gates: that your days may be multiplied, and the days of your children, in the land which the Lord sware unto your fathers to give them, as the days of heaven upon the earth" (Deuteronomy 11:18–21).

"And, ye fathers, provoke not your children to wrath: but bring them up in the nurture and admonition of the Lord" (Ephesians 6:4).

Paul felt it an advantage to Timothy, and helpful to the work in which he was engaged, that he had known the Holy Scriptures from a child. The writer feels very grateful to God that the New Testament was the first book that went into his soul, and went in early and opened the gates for Christ ere the evil day had come.

(f) To labor and give for the advancement of the gospel beyond her bounds.

(1) By contributing to schools for the preparation of pastors and teachers. We must have "workmen" who do not need to be ashamed of their efforts or afraid of the enemies of the truth. (2) By contributing to the support of missionary operations, both home and foreign, and for the diffusion of a pure Christian and Scriptural literature. Of course, the promotion of all these different objects calls for plans, conference, prayer, wisdom, and money; but the end to be gained, the bringing of many sons of God to glory, is worth the means demanded.

"Over the ocean wave, far, far away,
There the poor heathen live, waiting for day,
Groping in ignorance, dark as the night,
No blessed Bible to give them the light.
Pity them, pity them, Christians at home,
Haste with the bread of life, hasten and come."

The messengers of Christ in large numbers should be called by the church to "go unto the heathen," as did Paul and Barnabas (Galatians 2:9); and all that may be necessary to "bring them on their way" should be cheerfully supplied.

(5) THE DISCIPLINE OF A CHURCH

A church is a government, with its laws, officers, and subjects. Christ, as we have seen, is its Head, and the Bible is its code of laws. It is "a lamp unto the feet and a light unto the path" of the churches as well as of the separate members thereof. The pastor is overseer, and represents Christ in leading the church to apply the law to its members.

With regard to the discipline of the church, it is either "formative" or "corrective."

(a) Formative discipline has reference to the teaching of the doctrines and precepts of the gospel, that the church may increase or grow in the knowledge of the truth as it is in Jesus. God's word is a copy of his character. It implies constant, wise, and loving watchcare and training, that the members may grow up into the likeness of Christ, and that their powers of body, mind, and heart may be fitted for the services that they may be called to perform. In an army every soldier is thus taught and trained and exercised, in order that there may be no sluggard in action and no laggard on the march. A church that has had the benefit of wise and loving formative discipline is a beautiful sight to men and to angels, every member a help to all, and giving thus additional strength and increased success to the church in its work.

(b) Corrective discipline refers to those whose conduct has in some way been such as to need reproof and correction.

The church is to guard the truths that the Lord has entrusted to them; it is to be careful that the lives of the members are such as to bring no reproach on the Great Head of the Church; and that none of them introduces dissensions and mars the peace and harmony of the body. One sinner in the church, by the introduction of heresy, by an unholy life, by a contentious and unbrotherly spirit, may destroy much good. Hence, there is a need for the enforcement of Christian discipline.

Paul, in writing to the boastful church at Corinth, speaks with deep, but not unnecessary, earnestness:

"It is reported commonly *that there is* fornication among you, and such fornication as is not so much as named among the Gentiles, that one should have his father's wife. And ye are puffed up, and have not rather mourned, that he that hath done this deed might be taken away from among you. For I verily, as absent in body, but present in spirit, have judged already, as though I were present, *concerning* him that hath so done this deed, in the name of our Lord Jesus Christ, when ye are gathered together, and my spirit, with the power of our Lord Jesus Christ, to deliver such a one unto Satan for the destruction of the flesh, that the spirit may be saved in the day of the Lord Jesus. Your glorying is not good. Know ye not that a little leaven leaveneth the whole lump? Purge out therefore the old leaven, that ye may be a new lump, as ye are unleavened. ... But now I have written unto you not to keep company, if any man that is called a brother be a fornicator, or covetous, or an idolater, or a railer, or a drunkard, or an extortioner; with such a one no not to eat. For what have I to do to judge them also that are without? do not ye judge them that are within? But them that are without God judgeth. Therefore put away from among yourselves that wicked person" (1 Corinthians 5:1-7, 11-13).

From such as practice these and similar offenses, we are commanded to withdraw ourselves. The person referred to was excluded by the church, and was led to bitter repentance, as the following shows:

"For out of much affliction and anguish of heart I wrote unto you with many tears; not that ye should be grieved, but that ye might know the love which I have more abundantly unto you. ... Sufficient to such a man *is* this punishment, which *was inflicted* of many. So that contrariwise ye *ought* rather to forgive *him*, and comfort *him*, lest perhaps such a one should be swallowed up with overmuch sorrow. Wherefore I beseech you that ye would confirm *your* love toward him" (2 Corinthians 2:4, 6-8).

The Corinthian Church proved that it had no sympathy with this ugly crime, by cutting off the wicked person, nor do they allow him to return to their fellowship till months have passed, and even then he returns only on the signs of genuine repentance, sweetened and commended by the pleadings of the apostle. Paul writes to Titus:

"A man that is a heretic, after the first and second admonition, reject, knowing that he that is such is subverted, and sinneth, being condemned of himself" (Titus 3:10, 11).

To the Thessalonians he says:

"For even when we were with you, this we commanded you, that if any would not work, neither should he eat. For we hear that there are some which walk among you disorderly, working not at all, but are busybodies. Now them that are such we command and exhort by our Lord Jesus Christ, that with quietness they work, and eat their own bread. But ye, brethren, be not weary in well doing. And if any man obey not our word by this epistle, note that man, and have no company with him, that he may be ashamed" (2 Thessalonians 3:10-14).

All the cases mentioned here deserve correction, and must be corrected, and for the reason, as Paul says, that their poisonous leaven must be put out of the church, lest the whole body should degenerate and rot under its influence. The crimes are not of the same nature, and hence they deserve different treatment. If it be known to all that a man is guilty of one single act of adultery, or fornication, or murder, or wanton drunkenness, or deliberate cruelty, or malicious lying, or stealing, or false swearing, or of using profane language, the church must exclude the offender from her fellowship; for only in this way can she clear herself from the guilt of the offense and maintain her good name before the public to the honor of her Lord. And in the church, as elsewhere, the rule that sin must be punished still holds good.

"Them that sin rebuke before all, that others also may fear. I charge *thee* before God, and the Lord Jesus Christ, and the elect angels, that thou observe these things without preferring one before another, doing nothing by partiality" (1 Timothy 5:20, 21).

If it be known that a man is inclined to be a busybody, a heretic, or disturber of the faith and peace of the church, a covetous person, an extortioner, a tattler, an absentee from the public services of the church, a covenant breaker, he should be spoken to twice or thrice; and if he refuse to be corrected, he must be excluded. But in all cases kindness is demanded, and the law must be administered in a spirit of humility and love.

"Brethren, if a man be overtaken in a fault, ye which are spiritual, restore such a one in the spirit of meekness; considering thyself, lest thou also be tempted. Bear ye one another's burdens, and so fulfil the law of Christ. For if a man think himself to be something, when he is nothing, he deceiveth himself" (Galatians 6:1).

Three motives should rule us as we administer discipline—namely, the glory of God; the honor of the church; the good of the offender.

Personal offenses should be dealt with according to the plain directions that the Lord himself gave to his disciples while yet with them.

"Moreover if thy brother shall trespass against thee, go and tell him his fault between thee and him alone: if he shall hear thee, thou hast gained thy brother. But if he will not hear *thee, then* take with thee one or two more, that in the mouth of two or three witnesses every word may be established. And if he shall neglect to hear them, tell *it* unto the church: but if he neglect to hear the church, let him be unto thee as a heathen man and a publican" (Matthew 18:15–17).

"If thou bring thy gift to the altar, and there rememberest that thy brother hath aught against thee; leave there thy gift before the altar, and go thy way; first be reconciled to thy brother, and then come and offer thy gift. Agree with thine adversary quickly, while thou art in the way with him; lest at any time the adversary deliver thee to the judge, and the judge deliver thee to the officer, and thou be cast into prison. Verily I say unto thee, Thou shalt by no means come out thence, till thou hast paid the uttermost farthing" (Matthew 5:23-26).

The duties pointed out in these passages are binding upon both parties— the duty to seek reconciliation with each other. The offended seeks the offender, and the offender seeks the offended. How proper and how beautiful is this rule! Oh, that all would heed it!

> "More like Jesus would I be;
> Let my Saviour dwell in me,
> Fill my soul with peace and love,
> Make me gentle as a dove."

9

The Last Things

(1) DEATH

We are told by the Apostle Paul that all things are for the good of the saints—whether the world, or life, or death, or things present, or things to come—and they ought to utilize them as the busy bee utilizes the flower. Stored away in everything, there is something for those who love God, who are the called according to his purpose. After the fall, God said to Adam:

"In the sweat of thy face shalt thou eat bread, till thou return unto the ground; for out of it wast thou taken: for dust thou *art,* and unto dust shalt thou return" (Genesis 3:19).

And the Atonement has brought no change at this point. Still, "it is appointed unto men once to die." The way to the spirit world lies through this dark valley. As yet, only two have passed up another way. Jesus went through this gate on his way to "the right hand of the Majesty on high." I would observe:

(a) That it becomes us to prepare to meet death in such a way as to promote the glory of God and the triumph of the Christian faith. Look at the scenes which form the last chapters in the lives of Jacob, of Joseph, of Moses, of Joshua, of David, of Paul, of Peter, and of many others. Not a few, like Samson, have slain more of the opposition in their death than they slew in their lives. This idea of glorifying God in death is seen in Jesus' words to Peter at the sea of Galilee:

"This spake he, signifying by what death he should glorify God. And when he had spoken this, he saith unto him, Follow me" (John 21:19).

As a bold witness for Christ, choosing to die rather than deny him, he died glorifying him in his death.

Of late we hear of many who have taken their own lives and rushed unbidden into the presence of God, while others have been crazed by misfortunes or failures in business. Such things are not to the praise of the grace of God. Believers in Christ should never be driven by earthly troubles to such sin; for Jesus himself told his disciples:

"In the world ye shall have tribulation: but be of good cheer; for I have overcome the world" (John 16:33).

Troubles form an important part of that discipline which God, in his wisdom and grace, appoints to his people. Paul met with many on his way through life; but he was not cast down by them. Writing to the church at Corinth, he said:

"And lest I should be exalted above measure through the abundance of the revelations, there was given to me a thorn in the flesh, the messenger of Satan to buffet me, lest I should be exalted above measure. For this thing I besought the Lord thrice, that it might depart from me. And he said unto me, My grace is sufficient for thee: for my strength is made perfect in weakness. Most gladly therefore will I rather glory in my infirmities, that the power of Christ may rest upon me. Therefore I take pleasure in infirmities, in reproaches, in necessities, in persecutions, in distresses for Christ's sake: for when I am weak, then am I strong" (2 Corinthians 12:7–10).

Those who die under a cloud of sin—as did Solomon, the renowned son of David—and those who have been entrusted by God with worldly means, and have died without any reference to will as to the disposal of his property, and any apparent desire that the Lord's means should promote the Lord's work—such can scarcely be said to die to the glory of God. We should live, day by day, as though we constantly stood at the judgment seat, ready at a moment to leave the post of duty for the place of rest.

(b) We should free ourselves from the terrors of death. In a very striking picture, Paul brings the facts concerning death before us in the following verses:

"The sting of death is sin; and the strength of sin is the law. But thanks be to God, which giveth us the victory through our Lord Jesus Christ. Therefore, my beloved brethren, be ye steadfast, unmoveable, always abounding in the work of the Lord, forasmuch as ye know that your labour is not in vain in the Lord" (1 Corinthians 15:56, 57).

In this we see the form of some strong, stinging creature, the venom of whose sting has been taken away, and who is, therefore, harmless and no longer to be feared. Death was this creature; the law was the strength of sin which was Death's sting. The apostle rejoices that Christ had disabled the monster, leaving him without power, without sting. It is not strange, however, that, notwithstanding we may know that the hornet is weak and stingless, still his feeble buzzing makes us afraid. But let us settle it in our hearts that Christ is our victory.

(2) THE INTERMEDIATE STATE

For awhile we are to be separated from the body. We are not told why, but we may be sure that it is for some good purpose. This fact too, is a flower rich with sweet juices. We shall come out from thence with something new. While in that intermediate state we shall be both conscious and happy. The following shows that departed spirits are not asleep: We are told by the Lord of the removal of the rich man and Lazarus to the other world. The rich man in hell:

"Lifted up his eyes, being in torments, and seeth Abraham afar off, and Lazarus in his bosom. And he cried and said, Father Abraham, have mercy on me, and send Lazarus, that he may dip the tip of his finger in water, and cool my tongue; for I am tormented in this flame. But Abraham said, Son, remember that thou in thy lifetime receivedst thy good things, and likewise Lazarus evil things: but now he is comforted, and thou art tormented. And beside all this, between us and you there is a great gulf fixed: so that they which would pass from hence to you cannot; neither can they pass to us, that *would come* from thence" (Luke 16:23–26).

The departed saints are blessed, and interested in the work of the Lord in this world.

"Here is the patience of the saints: here *are* they that keep the command-ments of God, and the faith of Jesus. And I heard a voice from heaven *saying* unto me, Write, Blessed are the dead which die in the Lord from henceforth: Yea, saith the Spirit, that they may rest from their labours: and their works do follow them" (Revelation 14:12, 13).

"And after six days Jesus taketh Peter, James, and John his brother, and bringeth them up into a high mountain apart, and was transfigured before them: and his face did shine as the sun, and his raiment was white as the light. And, behold, there appeared unto them Moses and Elias talking with him. Then answered Peter, and said unto Jesus, Lord, it is good for us to be here: if thou wilt, let us make here three tabernacles; one for thee, and one for Moses, and one for Elias. While he yet spake, behold, a bright cloud overshadowed them: and behold a voice out of the cloud, which said, This is my beloved Son, in whom I am well pleased; hear ye him. And when the disciples heard *it*, they fell on their face, and were sore afraid" (Matthew 17:1–6).

Here are Moses and Elijah. The former had been dead over fourteen hundred years, the latter had gone to heaven in the chariot of fire about nine hundred years before this scene on the mount. That they were in full possession of all the attributes of personality, and in active consciousness, is plain in the fact that they appear as interested in Christ's death, which is the subject of their conversation with him.

During this period the saints are in heaven with Jesus. In proof of this statement, we have the following:

"I go to prepare a place for you. And if I go and prepare a place for you, I will come again, and receive you unto myself; that where I am, there ye may be also" (John 14:2, 3).

"I knew a man in Christ above fourteen years ago, (whether in the body, I cannot tell; or whether out of the body, I cannot tell: God knoweth;) such a one caught up to the third heaven. And I knew such a man, (whether in the body, or out of the body, I cannot tell: God knoweth;) how that he *was* caught up into paradise, and heard unspeakable words, which it is not lawful for a man to utter" (2 Corinthians 12:2–4).

During Paul's first imprisonment at Rome (Acts 28), and when it seemed probable that he would be put to death, the Christians at Philippi wrote him a letter of sympathy, and sent him a donation by Epaphroditus. In reply to this kindness, Paul writes these touching words:

"For me to live is Christ, and to die is gain. But if I live in the flesh, this is the fruit of my labour: yet what I shall choose I wot not. For I am in a strait betwixt two, having a desire to depart and to be with Christ; which is far better" (Philippians 1:21–23).

Very plainly it appears that "heaven," "third heaven," and "paradise" mean the same place. No doubt the disembodied saints are still busy in our spiritual affairs.

(3) THE RESURRECTION

This doctrine appears—

(a) In the Old Testament. Daniel says:

"And at that time shall Michael stand up, the great prince which standeth for the children of thy people: and there shall be a time of trouble, such as never was since there was a nation *even* to that same time: and at that time thy people shall be delivered, every one that shall be found written in the book. And many of them that sleep in the dust of the earth shall awake, some to everlasting life, and some to shame *and* everlasting contempt. And they that be wise shall shine as the brightness of the firmament; and they that turn many to righteousness, as the stars for ever and ever" (Daniel 12:1-3).

"As for me, I will behold thy face in righteousness: I shall be satisfied, when I awake, with thy likeness" (Psalm 17:15).

(b) In the New Testament the doctrine stands out as in noonday light. Inspiration gives us the following pen portraiture of that glorious event:

"But I would not have you to be ignorant, brethren, concerning them which are asleep, that ye sorrow not, even as others which have no hope. For if we believe that Jesus died and rose again, even so them also which sleep in Jesus will God bring with him. For this we say unto you by the word of the Lord, that we which are alive *and* remain unto the coming of the Lord shall not prevent them which are asleep. For the Lord himself shall descend from heaven with *a* shout, with the voice of the archangel, and with the trump of God: and the dead in Christ shall rise first: then we which are alive *and* remain shall be caught up together with them in the clouds, to meet the Lord in the air: and so shall we ever be with the Lord. Wherefore comfort one another with these words" (1 Thessalonians 4:13-18).

Here is a great mystery; but the body that shall be will be spiritual to suit its spiritual habitation and spiritual company.

"*There are* also celestial bodies, and bodies terrestrial; but the glory of the celestial is one, and the *glory* of the terrestrial *is* another. *There is* one glory of the sun, and another glory of the moon, and another glory of the stars; for *one* star differeth from *another* star in glory. So also *is* the resurrection of the dead. It is sown in corruption, it is raised in incorruption: it is sown in dishonour, it is raised in glory: it is sown in weakness, it is raised in power: it is sown a natural body, it is raised a spiritual body. There is a natural body, and there is a spiritual body. And so it is written, The first man Adam was made a living soul; the last Adam *was made* a quickening spirit. ... Behold, I shew you a mystery; We shall not all sleep, but we shall all be changed. In a moment, in the twinkling of an eye, at the last trump: for the trumpet shall sound, and the dead shall be raised incorruptible, and we shall be changed. For this corruption must put on incorruption, and this mortal *must* put on immortality. So when this corruptible shall have put on incorruption, and this mortal shall have put on immortality, then shall be brought to pass the saying that is written, Death is swallowed up in victory. O death, where *is* thy sting? O grave, where *is* thy victory?" (1 Corinthians 15).

Regarding the possibility of the resurrection, it is enough to say that it will be brought about by the almighty power, and in the infinite wisdom of God. Which is easier for God to do, to make a living soul, or to make forms in which to clothe it? Which is easier to do, to make a man or to make a house for him to live in? Said Jesus: "Ye do err, not knowing the power of God." Remember who it is that engages to bring about the resurrection, and all is plain. How precious the thought!

> "*Drawing nearer my home, every moment I am,*
> *Drawing nearer my home and the throne of the Lamb,*
> *Where the ties that were broken again shall unite,*
> *And our hearts shall be one in eternal delight.*"

(4) The general judgment

God has made clearly known to us that there is to be "the end of the world," and that when that end arrives all those who have dwelt in the world from the creation of Adam and Eve until the last born of men shall be called before the judgment seat of Christ. This end of the world was spoken of by Christ when he met his disciples on the mount in Galilee. After giving to them his Great Commission, he spoke words of gracious encouragement:

"Lo, I am with you alway, even unto the end of the world" (Matthew 28:20).

The Lord also made frequent mention of "that day," by which he evidently meant the same as "the last day," or the "end of the world." That "last day" was also to be a day of judgment.

"He that rejecteth me, and receiveth not my words, hath one that judgeth him: the word that I have spoken, the same shall judge him in the last day" (John 12:48).

There was also evidently a conviction that "the resurrection" and "the judgment" were to be at "the last day." See Martha's reply to Jesus.

"Martha saith unto him, I know that he shall rise again in the resurrection at the last day" (John 11:24).

The characteristics of that day become more fully set forth as time passes on. Paul, preaching on Mars Hill in Athens, said:

"And the times of this ignorance God winked at; but now commandeth all men every where to repent: because he hath appointed a day, in the which he will judge the world in righteousness by *that* man whom he hath ordained; *whereof* he hath *given* assurance unto all *men*, in that he hath raised him from the dead" (Acts 17:31).

It came to be frequently spoken of as "the day of wrath," "the day of the Lord Jesus," "the day of Jesus Christ," "the day of redemption," "the day of judgment." In one of the last few days of the Lord's teaching on earth, he gave the following graphic picture of that great day:

"When the Son of man shall come in his glory, and all the holy angels with him, then shall he sit upon the throne of his glory: and before him shall be gathered all nations: and he shall separate them one from another, as a shepherd divideth *his* sheep from the goats: and he shall set the sheep on his right hand, but the goats on the left. Then shall the King say unto them on his right hand, Come, ye blessed of my Father, inherit the kingdom prepared for you from the foundation of the world: for I was a hungered, and ye gave me meat: I was thirsty, and ye gave me drink: I was a stranger, and ye took me in: naked, and ye clothed me: I was sick, and ye visited me: I was in prison, and ye came unto me. ... Verily I say unto you, Inasmuch as ye have done *it* unto one of the least of these my brethren, ye have done *it* unto me. Then shall he say also unto them on the left hand, Depart from me, ye cursed, into everlasting fire, prepared for the devil and his angels: for I was a hungered, and ye gave me no meat: I was thirsty, and ye gave me no drink: I was a stranger, and ye took me not in: naked, and ye clothed me not: sick, and in prison, and ye visited me not. Verily I say unto you, Inasmuch as ye did *it* not to one of the least of these, ye did *it* not to me. And these shall go away into everlasting punishment: but the righteous into life eternal" (Matthew 25:31-36, 40-43, 45, 46).

It will be a day of righteous judgment when every one shall give account of himself to God. The apostle dwells on the righteousness of the judgment to be pronounced at that great day.

"But we are sure that the judgment of God is according to truth against them which commit such things. And thinkest thou this, O man, that judgest them which do such things, and doest the same, that thou shalt escape the judgment of God? Or despisest thou the riches of his goodness and forbearance and longsuffering; not knowing that the goodness of God leadeth thee to repentance? But after thy hardness and impenitent heart treasurest up unto thyself wrath against the day of wrath and revelation of the righteous judgment of God; who will render to every man according to his deeds: to them who by patient continuance in well doing seek for glory and honour and immortality, eternal life: but unto them that are contentious, and do not obey the truth, but obey unrighteousness, indignation and wrath, tribulation and anguish, upon every soul of man that doeth evil; of the Jew first, and also of the Gentile; but glory, honour, and peace, to every man that worketh good: to the Jew first, and also to the Gentile: for there is no respect of persons with God. For as many as have sinned without law shall also perish without law; and as many as have sinned in the law shall be judged by the law; (for not the hearers of the law *are* just before God, but the doers of the law shall be justified. For when the Gentiles, which have not the law, do by nature the things contained in the law, these, having not the law, are a law unto themselves: Which shew the work of the law written in their hearts, their conscience also bearing witness, and *their* thoughts the mean while accusing or else excusing one another;) in the day when God shall judge the secrets of men by Jesus Christ according to my gospel" (Romans 2:2–16).

John depicts the scene as beheld by him in prophetic vision:

"And I saw a great white throne, and him that sat on it, and from whose face the earth and the heaven fled away; there was found no place for them. And I saw the dead, small and great, stand before God; and the books were opened: and another book was opened, which is *the book* of life: and the dead were judged out of those things which were written in the books, according to their works. And the sea gave up the dead which were in it; and death and hell delivered up the dead which were in them: and they were judged every man according to their works" (Revelation 20:11–13).

What trembling shall take the world in that day on the one side, and what triumph and joy shall be on the other! What disappointments, what separations, what losses, what bitter memories, what self-accusations, what heartrending regrets, what despair and remorse, shall be seen in that day when it is said:

"He that is unjust, let him be unjust still: and he which is filthy, let him be filthy still: and he that is righteous, let him be righteous still: and he that is holy, let him be holy still" (Revelation 22:11).

Many would, if they could, flee to the dens and caves of the earth to hide from the face of the Lamb, whose love they have rejected.

(5) THE FINAL STATE OF THE LOST

It will be seen, from what has been said in regard to the judgment of the last day, that the decisions of that day are both spoken of as final; that is, the Judge speaks of the lost as though his decision left for them no hope, and of the saved as though for them there was no more fear. The state of each class is regarded as fixed beyond change.

Their final abode is depicted in fearful terms by the Lord himself, who pronounces the dreadful sentence on the lost:

"Depart from me, ye cursed, into everlasting fire prepared for the devil and his angels" (Matthew 25:41).

This dark and fearful abode was prepared for Satan and the angels that followed him, and thus kept not their first estate:

"And the angels which kept not their first estate, but left their own habitation, he hath reserved in everlasting chains under darkness unto the judgment of the great day. Even as Sodom and Gomorrah, and the cities about them in like manner, giving themselves over to fornication, and going after strange flesh, are set forth for an example, suffering the vengeance of eternal fire" (Jude 6, 7).

Its horror comes from the following sources:

(a) A consciousness of being possessed of incurable, self-imposed moral pollution.

(b) A consciousness of deserved punishment.

(c) A consciousness of a hopeless loss of the last proffered mercy or extended means of deliverance.

(d) A fearful sense of endless bondage and everlasting confinement.

(e) A sense of utter helplessness, with no hope of ever again securing the ear of the once-gracious Judge.

(f) The memory of lost opportunities and past blessings.

(g) The fearful company of demons and of all who have forgotten God.

(h) The displeasure of the Lord Jehovah.

It is described as a "lake that burns with fire and brimstone," as an "outer darkness where there is wailing and gnashing of teeth." Hearken!

"He that overcometh shall inherit all things; and I will be his God, and he shall be my son. But the fearful, and unbelieving, and the abominable, and murderers, and whoremongers, and sorcerers, and idolaters, and all liars, shall have their part in the lake which burneth with fire and brimstone: which is the second death" (Revelation 21:7, 8).

"Whosoever was not found written in the book of life was cast into the lake of fire" (Revelation 20:15).

Oh, that men would strive to shun this woeful end! As we stand and gaze upon such woes, and think of their endless duration, the soul sickens and the spirit faints.

(6) THE FINAL STATE OF THE SAVED

Here let us relieve our heavy hearts with a song:

> *"Oh, sweet and blessed country,*
> *The home of God's elect!*
> *Oh, sweet and blessed country,*
> *That eager hearts expect!*
> *Jesus, in mercy, bring us*
> *To that dear land of rest,*
> *Who art, with God the Father*
> *And Spirit, ever blest."*

With what sweet relief we view the end of our earthly wanderings, our sore sorrows and bitter toil! With what ecstatic, unspeakable joy we come in sight of the "house of many mansions," the "far more exceeding and eternal weight of glory!"

Heaven is the home of the divine family, the "house of many mansions." In it there is nothing to defile, nothing to hinder, nothing to mar, nothing to grieve, nothing to disturb, nothing to distress, nothing to worry, nothing to give pain, nothing to cause fear, no danger of falling. There is no need of candle, of lamp, of stars, of moon, of sun to give light therein; for "there is no night there"—none, because God and the Lamb are there, and because the glory of God does eternally light up that happy land.

The joy of the saints will forever increase from these sources:

(a) From the presence and love of God the Father, and the Son, and the Holy Spirit.

(b) A sense of perfect personal holiness.

(c) A recollection of the depth from whence they came up, and the way they came.

(d) A sight of the grace by which they were saved.

(e) Their entire restoration to the likeness and favor of God.

(f) A sense of their endless and perfect freedom.

(g) The blessedness of their habitation.

(h) Their sinless and peaceable association.

(i) Their unfailing youth and ever-increasing strength in all that is great, good, and glorious.

(j) The bliss of their glorious engagements.

(k) The company of loved ones who went from the earth. There those long parted meet again, to part no more forever.

(l) The good will and great love of our God.

And here we let John close with a picture from his wondrous vision:

"And he showed me a pure river of water of life, clear as crystal, proceeding out of the throne of God and of the Lamb. In the midst of the street of it, and on either side of the river, *was there* the tree of life, which bare twelve *manner* of fruits, *and* yielded her fruit every month: and the leaves of the tree *were* for the healing of the nations. And there shall be no more curse: but the throne of God and of the Lamb shall be in it; and his servants shall serve him: and they shall see his face; and his name *shall be* in their foreheads. And there shall be no night there; and they need no candle, neither light of the sun; for the Lord God giveth them light: and they shall reign for ever and ever. And he said unto me, These sayings *are* faithful and true: and the Lord God of the holy prophets sent his angel to shew unto his servants the things which must shortly be done. Behold, I come quickly: blessed *is* he that keepeth the sayings of the prophecy of this book. And I John saw these things, and heard *them*. And when I had heard and seen, I fell down to worship before the feet of the angel which shewed me these things. Then saith he unto me, See *thou do it not*: for I am thy fellow servant, and of thy brethren the prophets, and of them which keep the sayings of this book: worship God. And he saith unto me, Seal not the sayings of the prophecy of this book: for the time is at hand" (Revelation 22:1–10).

"By-and-by, when the reapers come,
    And we hear the song of the harvest home,
    'Twill be sweet to think of our labors done,
    Of the golden sheaves in the setting sun.

"By-and-by, when at home we meet,
    When we cast our sheaves at the Master's feet,
    In the land of rest 'twill be joy to know
    It was not in vain that we toiled below.

"By-and-by, if we watch and wait,
    We shall enter in at the pearly gate:
    We shall sit us down with our friends above,
    'Mid the songs of joy, in a feast of love."

THE END

— General Index

– *Scripture Index*

OLD TESTAMENT

NEW TESTAMENT